D1519476

PART 1

1

IF THERE WAS ANYTHING especially dramatic about Joe DeLude, nobody ever knew what it was. Nor had he any very close resemblance to Adonis. He was broad of rump and well upholstered around the middle. But as a ship's tailor he was a ball of fire. Joe, whose home was in Maine and who derived from thrifty French-Canadian stock, had been patching and altering clothes on the light cruiser *Marblehead* for fourteen years. He could do as neat a job with a sewing machine as most tailors can by the most painstaking hand stitching. And while almost all sailors are inveterate buyers of foreign-made curios and junk, Joe bought only fine linens that had been elegantly embroidered. Being a connoisseur in such matters, he knew exactly how much work had gone into each piece and usually managed to get a little more than his money's worth. That was very important to Joe, who always had a nice warm feeling for a dollar bill. If circumstances ever demanded it, he could, on his return to the States, sell these linens at an interesting profit. But a part of them were very definitely earmarked for his little sister.

Joe was fortyish, childless and wifeless, so that his feeling for his sister, who was twenty years younger, was much more that of a father than a brother. And now that this somewhat unusual love affair had materialized between his sister and one of his shipmates, Joe felt that she'd soon probably be setting up housekeeping and would need linens, even though Joe and her swain were at the moment plugging along through the Java Sea on an obsolescent cruiser, many thousands of miles from home.

The fact that a political situation of considerable tension now existed between the United States and the Japanese government was not causing Joe to lose any sleep. If there was a war, he'd have his own hands full keeping his shipmates properly dressed.

It was the admirals' job to do the worrying. If not, why was there such a large difference between their pay and his?

As a matter of fact, Admiral Tommy Hart, as commander of the Asiatic Fleet, would probably have agreed with Joe, and, during this November of 1941, he was certainly trying to earn his pay. The admiral had already eased his ships out to sea for strategic dispersal. For while Pearl Harbor was over 5,000 miles from Tokyo, Manila was only half that distance, and manifestly a dangerous place to be caught with a heavy concentration of ships in a sneak air raid.

It was on Admiral Hart's orders that as early as November 27th the *Marblehead*'s skipper, Captain A. G. Robinson, while still at sea, had told his executive officer, Commander W. B. Goggins, to publish in the ship's plan of the day that all outgoing mail would henceforth be censored. The ship would be making port in a couple of days and, owing to the political crisis, no one must be allowed to give away her position. Censorship had been unnecessary until now, inasmuch as none of the crew knew the ship's destination.

Did the captain wish to nominate a censorship officer?

"How about Ensign Bracken?" the captain suggested.

The captain thought about John Bracken because he liked him. John was a big handsome lad who shared the captain's appreciation of a good party. Also, because Ensign Bracken had a rather exact sense of decorum, and good taste in all matters from music to naval etiquette, he'd become the ship's secretary and, when necessary, the captain's social stand-in.

Commander Goggins thought John Bracken a fine selection for censorship officer, but for a different reason: it was against his religion to see a junior officer have too much spare time. Commander Goggins was one of those senior officers who feel that if his junior officers don't all ultimately become skippers, and good ones too, the fault lies with the way they were brought up in the fleet. In or out of the Navy, he would have had a hawk's eye for precise detail. In the presence of a

Where Away

Contents

Where Away

The Story of the U.S.S. Marblehead

George Sessions Perry

Isabel Leighton

Copyright

Where Away: The Story of the U.S.S. Marblehead by George Sessions Perry and Isabel Leighton. First published in 1944.

Hardcover edition published by Ship to Shore Books, 2022.

This book or any portion thereof may not be scanned, digitized, reproduced or used in any manner whatsoever without the express written permission of the publisher except for the use of brief quotations in a book review or scholarly journal. All rights reserved.

First printing: 2022.

ISBN: 9798836077853.

slipshod junior officer, he could be nasty when he wanted to and, every now and again, he wanted to. When well out of his hearing, his shipmates often referred to him as Sergeant York because his lanky figure, in loose-legged white uniform shorts, plus a vaguely ducklike gait, called to mind that World War I backwoods hero.

When the new censorship rule was posted, on the morning of the 28th, the mystification and burning curiosity of the crew were only intensified. The enlisted men constantly watched the officers for any revealing slip regarding the ship's destination. If rail-thin M. J. Drury, the First Lieutenant, happened to make a check of the ship's heavy foul-weather clothing, the word went abroad that the ship's probable destination was Alaska or Vladivostok. If Lt. Commander Zern, the navigator, asked one of the men in the chart house for a chart of the Bay of Bengal, the ship was headed, on waves of scuttlebutt, for India.

But of course, the source of the best scuttlebutt is always the mess boys who serve the wardroom officers. As the serving tray is extended between the seated officers, what is to prevent two sharp ears from picking up all sorts of clues, especially when those ears are privileged to sample each conversation at the table as many times as there are courses served?

On the *Marblehead*, the mess boys were Chinese. But as the crew plied these men with questions, there was one that they left strictly alone, a sullen lad named Fook Liang. He had been ostracized ever since the day he had been directed to remove some hammocks from the crew's quarters and had refused on the grounds that he had joined the ship to serve officers and that to do anything for enlisted men was beneath him and would amount to a loss of face. Naturally, he was loathed by all the enlisted men who had heard this story, and all of them had.

But even the mess boys were unable to deliver the information so assiduously sought. The crew remained in ignorance of the ship's destination until, on November 29th, over the telephone circuit to the bridge-talker came, "Bridge Forward lookout—land dead ahead—looks like high land beyond the horizon."

A little later, even those without glasses could see the hills of Borneo looming up ahead and, still later, the lightship off Tarakan Roads. Because of the mirage effect that existed, it took, in succession, the shape of a low black blur, several detached black strata, one above the other, the shape of a sail, and finally after several other shifts unmistakably became the lightship. From seaward, the island of Tarakan, which lay just off the coast of Borneo, appeared to be only a couple of scattered clearings and a building or two in the flat, jungle-covered land behind which rose the jungle-covered hills. But when the ship, in the hands of a local pilot, had passed through the minefields and well into the harbor, the little town of Linkas with its oil tanks and docks was visible.

If the men needed proof of the political tension in the Pacific as November 1941 drew to a close, they had only to see the cables strung along the beaches, forming barriers to repel landing parties, or the pillboxes scattered beyond the barriers.

Before any liberty parties left the ship, the following bulletin was posted:

TARAKAN ROADS, BORNEO
NETHERLANDS INDIES

The town of Linkas is the only town on Tarakan Island. It is a rather small town with limited facilities for amusement and shopping. It is not known at this time just what recreation facilities will be available. Do not lose sight of the fact that this is a foreign port, and that you are here as a guest of a nation that is, at present, engaged in war.

Suggestions:

1. Do not associate with natives.

2. Do not be inquisitive about any restricted areas.

3. Most Dutchmen you see will be able to speak English. Do not attempt to speak Malay with anyone but natives.

4. No cameras nor firearms may be taken ashore.

5. Fresh provisions are apparently scarce; be careful of what you eat and drink.

6. The medium of exchange is the guilder, worth about fifty cents. An attempt will be made to have guilders available for exchange on board. American money will not be accepted ashore.

When the men went ashore, they found that everybody had war jitters. The people on Tarakan were sure it would be one of the first places the Japanese would attack, should war come to this part of the world. There wasn't much of a town, but as a fueling port and oil-producing center it was strategically important, since it and Balikpapan, a little farther south, were the only such ports on the Borneo coast.

At nightfall Tarakan was completely blacked out. The town was plastered with the jut-jawed visage of Winston Churchill, host of the Dutch government in exile. Even so, there was some coolness between the *Marblehead*'s enlisted men and the Dutch until Captain Robinson had one of his junior officers write and post an historical sketch which made it entirely clear that the Dutch and the Germans were not the same. After that, things went better except for the local wars that occurred when Shipfitter Second Class Clarence Aschenbrenner went ashore and anointed his cavernous insides with the various exotic potions for sale in Tarakan's bars.

"The Bull," as Aschenbrenner was called by his shipmates, hailed from New Ulm, Minnesota. He stood five feet six inches tall, had a shoulder spread of about a yard, the exuberance of a child, and the muscular development and power of a grizzly bear. Aboard ship he always did at least two men's work, did it well, with initiative and character, and loved doing it. He was convinced that there was no more honorable or enviable job than being a bluejacket in the United States Navy. He was so brimming with power and a kind of innocent, spontaneous pleasure that it spilled over on and infected the men who worked with him.

When he went ashore, he partook of spirits in the same grand and wholesale manner that he did everything else. And inevitably there came a point in his exhilaration when he could no longer restrain himself from having fun with that monumental strength of his. The Bull's barroom athletics never involved just one or two individuals. He loved to come to grips with veritable hordes of opponents, the number being limited only by the size of the saloon.

The Shore Patrol had reconnaissance groups to keep an eye on the Bull, in order that the main body could, in the hope of circumventing international complications, reach the scene of carnage ahead of the local constabulary.

Because if enough people of strange nationality set upon the Bull with nightsticks, he might lose his temper in a large way, and no one cared to visualize the devastation that would ensue. But a whole squad of the Shore Patrol, if they got there in time to handle things judiciously, could usually get the Bull back to the ship without anybody being permanently maimed. Then, after one of these titanic struggles, it was with a kind of sickness of heart that the Shore Patrol faced the necessity of putting the Bull on report. They knew there was no real harm in him. They loved him and were proud of him, and they realized that a part of that pride emanated from the godlike way in which he could eviscerate a barroom.

2

At Tarakan, the Bull's excursions into sprightly mayhem were less a problem than usual. For by Friday, December 5th, the news came that the Japanese had rejected the American demands. All liberty was canceled immediately. The ship was put on half-hour notice for getting underway. Captain Robinson told Commander Van Bergen, the gunnery officer, to put all guns on five minutes' notice.

Over Commander Nick Van Bergen's weathered face there was a patina of experience, the fruit not only of years at sea but of honest solitude and introspection, plus the stamp of quiet, implacable decision. In the fullest and most absolute sense of the term, Van Bergen, forty-three and a bachelor, was a Navy idealist. He had never seen a minute's action. Yet the concept of duty and responsibility and military character meant so much to him that he could hardly have continued as a naval officer, a part of whose duty is to die, if need be, with dignity, without having rehearsed that scene coldly and realistically in his own mind many times and having been confident that he knew his cues and his lines.

But that, though more or less the core of him, was by no means a full bill of particulars. In addition to what amounted to this wedding to the Navy, he was an outstandingly shrewd man.

Like all adroit military leaders, he could look at a man, see what treatment was required to produce the desired result, and then proceed to bind that man's allegiance to him. The treatment was almost always successful. By his extraordinary force of personality he could frequently correct a seaman in such a way that the culprit was: (1) glad he'd been corrected, (2) determined never to make that mistake again, and (3) somehow amazed at Van Bergen's forbearance.

Among the officers he was admired for his knowledge of his job and his careful attention to detail. And almost all of them were usually pervaded by the illusion that they were on terms of considerable intimacy with him.

But there was an interior Van Bergen that nobody would ever know. The only thing of which anyone could ever be certain about him was that he'd never be either foolish or emotionally sloppy in any of his naval duties or in battle, despite its outcome. These were the only open commitments he cared to make, and these, by anyone who was associated with him, were accepted at face value and as gilt-edged.

On his tour of inspection that Friday morning, December 5th, Commander Van Bergen found every gun ready to fire and all stations manned from the magazine crews in the bottom of the ship to the powder passers in the barbettes, which were the lightly armored vertical sleeves through which ammunition rose to the twin mounts, where powder and shell were rammed home into the guns by the loading crews.

The fact that the *Marblehead*'s ten 6-inch guns were distributed over the ship in a somewhat unusual manner made the gunnery officer's inspection trip longer than it would have been if the guns had been more conventionally arranged in three or four turrets swinging on the center line of the main deck. Instead, more or less like all her sisters of the *Omaha*-class, the ship had a twin mount on the forecastle, a single mount on each side of the base of the bridge structures, and two more single mounts above and slightly inboard of these.

On the stern there was another twin mount in the center of the fantail, and a single mount projecting on either hand from the after housing. The purpose and advantage of this wide dispersal of ordnance was simply that of not putting all of one's eggs in one basket. This way the *Marblehead* might have several guns knocked out of action, and yet retain something to fight with.

The disadvantage of such an arrangement was that, in combat with a single opponent, the ship could not conceivably be maneuvered so that all her guns would bear on the target.

The last of the main battery stations that Commander Van Bergen visited was the after-twin mount. Here Turret Captain Paul Martinek reported that his guns were ready and that that noise from somewhere lower in the barbette was not a steam leak but Seaman Harry Blackwell whistling a tune called Boogie Woogie Bugle Boy.

Van Bergen inspected the A.A. stations, in company with the air defense officers, Lt. R. G. Gillette, who, of course, was referred to among the enlisted men as "Blades," and sharp, temperamental Lt. Charles L. Browning. All the guns were found to be in shooting shape, tools and spares at hand and ready boxes full of ammunition. Exposed personnel had steel helmets and kapok life jackets, which the British had found to be good against tiny bomb fragments and splinters. Because of the structure of the ship, the ammunition trains could not, according to modern standards, move with any very real efficiency. But insofar as was possible, everything was now in readiness. The *Marblehead* was poised for the Japanese to do their worst.

Nor was anyone depressed by the fact that the Asiatic fleet at this time consisted only of the *Marblehead*, the *Houston*, thirteen old destroyers, a few submarines, gunboats, minesweepers, PTs, and auxiliaries. For all hands were convinced that once the Japanese threw down the gauntlet, powerful squadrons of the mighty United States Navy would steam out of Pearl Harbor and swell the tiny Asiatic Fleet to a thing of majesty and indomitable retribution.

3

On Saturday, December 6th, Chief Boatswain Harvey Andersen put his deck force through a fast workout, cleaning ship and making small repairs. He'd already been warned by Mr. Drury to have the ship in such condition that she could be further stripped quickly for action. (She had already been partially stripped months earlier in Manila.) Besides, later in the morning, Captain Robinson would make his weekly inspection of the entire ship. And this week particularly, if anything were not shipshape, those sharp gray-blue eyes of his would pick it up.

Viewed from the standpoint of a casting director seeking someone to symbolize every C.P.O. in the Navy, Chief Bos'n Andersen, now a chief warrant officer but lately of the ranks, had one grave fault: he was insufficiently pot-bellied. This does not mean that the equatorial areas of his torso were by any means the flat and barren plane of a stripling. But he certainly had not the brave bulge that might have been expected of one who had so lately been a chief petty officer, a rank which often connoted the most luxurious living of any group of officers aboard ship. It is true that the C.P.O. quarters back in the ship's narrow canoe-like stern were, while thoroughly comfortable, not as lavish as those of the skipper, but it certainly doesn't follow that the C.P.O.'s didn't eat as well and more. For though their food comes from the general mess, they can be depended upon to see that ample extras are at hand.

On any naval vessel the real power and respect that the C.P.O.'s command is not altogether unlike that which the lords of the realm had in feudal times in relation to the kings. In the first place they know more Navy than most "fresh-caught" junior officers, and they learned it not out of books but on a pitching ship. They are persons of force and character, or they would not have attained this absolute pinnacle of eminence in the enlisted man's scheme of things.

In their messroom, erudite conversations regarding the depth of Baffin Bay, the length of piston thrust in the reciprocating engines of any of the older World War I battlewagons, the rate scale on amorous consolation, plus names and addresses, in almost any port as of any specific year in the last twenty, the size, location, and number of guns on any fighting ship on the high seas, and a hundred other naval subjects, including exact details of any sea battle ever fought, are normal fare.

But to return to the casting director's view of Chief Bos'n Andersen, only the paunch failed to fill the composite picture of the representative C.P.O. The rest was all there: heavy black eyebrows, broad mustache, chin and jaw the shape, size and malleability of a horseshoe—plus a microscopically thorough knowledge of his job.

It was to instill this same thoroughness that Warrant Electrician Walter Jarvis had earlier seen to it that his electrician's mates had labeled and tagged with colored metal bands every electrical cable in the ship; tagged them not in one place but in every passageway and compartment where the circuits passed through, so that in case of trouble there would be no nameless cables strewn about starting fires and heightening confusion. Warrant Officer Jarvis was five feet and three inches of serious, careful, practical engineering knowledge. He had come into the Navy sixteen years earlier as a boot and had risen to his present rank during the promotion-scarce doldrums between two wars. Any of the men who'd ever served with him would tell you that there was not a better warrant electrician in the United States Navy or any other.

He had not of course undertaken this ambitious program of cable-labeling without first having received the approbation of Lt. Commander Camp, the engineering officer, who was his boss just as Drury was Chief Bos'n Andersen's, since Mr. Drury, as ship's First Lieutenant, was in charge of all maintenance and repair. Mr. Drury was, moreover, of the opinion that men could not be too well drilled in the matter of damage control. In fact, his zeal in this direction sometimes made the captain wonder how the carpenter and repair people could endure so much drill without going slightly crazy.

But Warrant Officer Jarvis and Chief Bos'n Andersen were not the only ones busily preparing for that Saturday morning inspection. Ever since the preceding afternoon, sailors had been bringing in clothes to the tailor shop to get Joe DeLude to make minor repairs. The fact that he was swamped with work just before an inspection was no surprise to Joe, who'd spent nineteen of his thirty-eight years at sea. Each year he'd picked up a little more weight, and each of the fifty-two weekly inspections of those years had found him covered up with work. Now, as his thick right arm pulled the needle away from the cloth with an abrupt, fast motion that made it look as if the thread would be snapped in two, he suddenly burst into alleged song, something Chinese which was principally monotone and filled the whole forward end of the ship. The fellows who were congregated in the barbershop looked at each other, and Hawkins, the barber, said, "Somebody has either got one of the mess boys hemmed up with a hatchet or Joe DeLude has run his hand into the sewing machine."

One had only to look at the windrows of hair on the deck to see that Hawkins had had a busy morning. Yet what made the little barbershop so crowded was that even after the men were shorn, if they had no immediate duty, they hung around to listen to Hawkins bat the breeze and crack wise.

The general theme upon which Hawkins held forth was sports: wrestling, boxing, baseball, billiards, bowling, track. He was an expert on all these subjects. He not only could but would tell you who played third base for the Cubs in 1913 and what his batting average was at the end of the season. If anybody cared to challenge any of his statements, he'd bet that he was right and, once the mahogany had been decorated, would drag out a dog-eared World Almanac and read the bad news to the party of the second part. As a matter of fact, an appreciable part of his income derived from this and affiliated sources, one of which was betting on baseball and football games. Hawkins had long since come to see that most of the fellows who hung around the barbershop had their analytical ability somewhat clouded by a kind of sectional patriotism, or boosterism. If a man had been born in St. Louis and the Cards were losing two games out of three, the St. Louis man's earthly treasures would, in a short course of time, find their way into Hawkins' pocket. It was the same with men from all sections. And there was one man who'd bet on Cincinnati even if the team consisted of only seven men.

Sometimes when there were several people on each side of the question, the bets would rise to as much as two hundred and fifty dollars on a World Series. Also, whenever a World Series was in progress, Hawkins usually operated the pool in which his shipmates bought tickets bearing the names of various players. The sailor holding the name of the player who got the most hits won the pot—after, that was, a reasonable amount had been deducted by Hawkins for his service.

He was one of those slight men who by reason of their smallness must confine their interest in athletics largely to the intellectual aspects thereof. He gave thoughtful and copious advice to Gunner Clendenin and Chief Bos'n's Mate Herman Hock, who usually managed and trained the ship's boxers, wrestlers, and baseball team. Sometimes Hawkins lay awake at night brooding and sorrowing over the fact that Metalsmith Martin Moran had "glass hands." Because, but for this heartbreaking and irreparable fact, he felt sure that he and Clendenin and Hock together could make Moran the heavyweight champion of the Asiatic Fleet and, of course, at the same time thereby ensure their own immortality.

Just now, however, Hawkins was laying down the law to the seamen who at the moment composed his gallery. "Comes a quarter to ten," he said, "you guys got to get out so I can clean the place up." And as that time came near, they melted away so that they too could get squared away to stand inspection.

Down in the sickbay, one deck below, Dr. Frank F. Wildebush, the senior medical officer, looked the place over in advance of the skipper's arrival and found that Archie Evans, Chief Pharmacist's Mate, whom everyone called "Ace," had everything under orderly control. Ace was a fullback-sized ex-West Coast footballer who ran the sickbay for the doctors and who, though he waited for the doctors to prescribe, could cure athlete's foot with his left hand and could recognize and slay a spirochete in the middle of the night with both eyes closed.

Dr. T. C. Ryan, the junior surgeon, was a slender, serious man in his early thirties with sandy hair and a thin reddish mustache. He had looked over the patients this morning and Pharmacist's Mate Starling Harold had seen to it that the bed cases had been bathed and given fresh linen. While the medical corps waited for the Chief Master-at-Arms to precede and announce the inspection party, Dr. Ryan dropped into the dental office to pass the time of day with Connie Brandt, the dental officer.

Connie got talking about the sailors in the forward repair party, some of whom were stationed in the sickbay during General Quarters. Also stationed there were some pharmacist's mates and stretcher-bearers, who, Brandt said, were usually studying first aid while they stood by, but the others were more given to lurid conversation. Connie told Dr. Ryan about one morning at General Quarters when the forward repair boys had been discussing how short the ship's small stores was of dungarees. One seemingly disinterested soul had pointed out that if war started, maybe the first battle would remedy the clothing shortage. All anybody would have to do, he'd said, would be to get clothes from the lockers of the men who wouldn't be needing them anymore. "And what if one of them happens to be you?" Connie had asked. "Well, if a shell pushes me through the bulkhead," the sailor had said, "the other guys are certainly welcome to anything they can find in my locker." Another lad had remarked on how nice it would be to collect so many pairs of shoes that he'd even have good "liberty" shoes to work in.

Dr. Ryan smiled. "We may get a chance before long to see how bloodthirsty they really are," he said.

Just then, "Ed" Edmondson, the Chief Master-at-Arms, called, "Attention!"

The inspection party was entering the sickbay. Dr. Ryan went to his station.

4

As the inspection party progressed from one department of the ship to another, Captain Robinson's eye caught rust that was forming in concealed corners or the absence of gaskets in hose nozzles. But he also noticed the little extra touches that had taken the last wrinkle out of the cover on a bunk, the last tinge of grease from the crevices of the broad iron plateau of galley stove, the carefully braided ends of bits of lines, that his men, after they had brought their stations to a condition of adequate cleanliness and order, had added in a simple and straightforward desire to please him.

The men of the *Marblehead* did not simply respect the skipper; they loved him. He had, and they all knew he had, deep consideration and a kind of automatic affection for every man in his crew. But they were men, and tough men, and had he not had character, ability and confidence, they could not have had this feeling of affection and trust. For men at sea are, it goes without saying, highly dependent upon the judgment, knowledge and courage of their skipper. To be a skipper in the United States Navy is a position of great eminence, and while in many ways Navy crews are both sentimental and somehow mystical, they are yet, by necessity, the most utilitarian of people. Untutored courage of the sort where a man, even at great risk to himself, makes some well-intentioned mistake that endangers the ship is despised. At sea, respect from a man's shipmates derives from a thorough knowledge of the duties signified by his rank. When a man has that knowledge, the foundations of respect have been laid. And then, as in the case of Captain Robinson, elements of character and personality come into the picture.

Some people could never look at Captain Robinson without being reminded of George M. Cohan, himself a man of great character, generosity, ability, and huge decency, whom his countrymen have seldom been able to view without affection. And if Mr. Cohan had ever been a sea captain, perhaps he would have been very much the same sort of seafaring man as Captain Arthur Granville Robinson of the *Marblehead*.

By 11:30 Captain Robinson and his department heads had made the rounds of the ship, and everybody began to take it easy. Everybody, that is, except the mess men, who were now scurrying from galley to mess tables with their stainless steel, multi-compartmented tureens, writing the menu of the impending meal along the passageways with the aroma from their containers. That menu was, of course, a foregone conclusion: the traditional Saturday ham and boiled vegetables, which had gone on cooking without attention while the ship's cooks stood inspection. In fact, boiled ham, cabbage and potatoes was such a fixture on the menu for Saturday noon that it had long since given rise to a little fable about the time when this menu had been served on Wednesday and half the ship had gone AWOL for twenty-four hours, thinking that the next day surely must be Sunday.

During the torpid afternoon, spontaneous bull sessions and a few covert crap games came into being. Scores of men simply crawled into their "sacks," as Navy bunks are called, and slept. Some of the old hands occupied themselves by braiding fancy belts out of linen line, belts with all sorts of designs, some with the names of girls interwoven for the women they were remembering and others without names to be stored as wampum against the requirements of the future. And as the steamy afternoon thickened into night, men off duty congregated on the weather deck, looked over the blacked-out town, thought of internally lighted bars and clubs, and reached the unanimous decision that this was a hell of a way to spend Saturday night.

Not that this was the first blackout the *Marblehead* men had seen. The first one back in Manila had caught some of the crew in a local refuge-for-the-thirsty known as Jake's Place, as was later brought out at captain's mast. When Bull Aschenbrenner, the first of the accused, had been brought before the captain, he had said, "Captain, sir, we all like Jake, so we go there a lot. Well, this was the first night of the try-out blackout. We went in and the lights were out, and it was pretty dark. No light anywhere except one candle on the end of the bar. Well, Bill comes in and slaps Jake on the back, and Jake thinks somebody's trying to take a poke at him, so Jake takes a swing at him. Bill falls back on a table where a couple of sailors are with some girls. One sailor picks up a chair and throws it at Bill because he was so clumsy and careless, but it misses Bill and hits the mirror at the back of the bar and smashes all the glasses and bottles. And, Captain, nobody was mad at nobody, but everybody starts slugging everybody else."

The next three witnesses had given almost identical testimony. Finally, the captain got to the last man, a quiet little fellow. The captain had said to him, "And what about you? Can you throw any additional light on the subject?"

"Honest, Captain," he said, "there wasn't no light to throw—only one little bittee candle."

Captain Robinson had barely been able to choke out, "Mast dismissed." And nothing was done to anyone.

Now, here at Tarakan, were more Japanese-inspired blackouts. If the Japs wanted to fight, why didn't they go on and start it and get it over with? This business of blacked-out towns and canceled liberty was taking all the fun out of being in the Navy. As it was, there was nothing to do but sit around and listen to the admonitory sermons of the Deacon, a lanky, country-bred seaman second class, whose ambition was one day to make chaplain, but who for the present served as a hot-shell-man on one of the 3-inch A.A.'s. Tonight, he held forth on the iniquitous aspects of tobacco, drink, and two-guilder Borneo whores.

Men who had the boiler and engine room duty felt they were somehow ahead of the game. It was not so bad to be stuck with the duty when nobody could go ashore anyway. But it was hot below, and when the men stayed too long beneath the relatively cool air of the ventilators, a chief petty officer came along and told them to mind their valves and gauges, that of all the times that a dreamy water-tender might select to blow up the ship, this, due to the political situation, was one of the least appropriate. And at this reference to the imminence of war, the thought of torpedoes pelting through the water and into the side of the ship was vivid in the minds of the men. They thought of the inferno of fire and steam and blood that would result.

"Suppose we got a fish in our guts?" the chief asked. "What would you guys do?"

"Get knocked off, I guess," one man said despondently.

"Oh, my God," the chief said. "I mighta known you'd do something useless. How about you, Sam?"

"Size things up, I guess, then try to duck the steam and get my fires out if the boilers were really broke up bad."

"Well, that's a little more like it." Then looking back at the first man, the chief said, "Jesus! You guys that are always getting knocked off. How does the Old Man expect me to keep those pots fired with shark bait…" And he turned and walked to the other end of the fire room with the easy-come easy-go disgust of a C.P.O., U.S.N.

5

Sunday, December 7th was just another wilting, hot, humid day in which everybody was under the sedative effect of too much fried chicken and ice cream. Lt. R. R. Hay, of Marblehead, Massachusetts, and Lt. Hepburn Pierce sat around Ensign Bracken's room listening to a concert of classical records and were soothed and excited by the rich vibrance of Marian Anderson's Ave Maria. Many of the men tried to write home, but there was always the annoying, as yet unassimilated consciousness of the censor's peering eye. This batch of letters was the least loving and intimate and spontaneous of any that had so far been posted in the *Marblehead*'s little post office, where H. M. Percifield, a Bos'n's Mate who doubled as mail clerk, dispensed stamps, sacked mail, dreamed great Nelson-like dreams, and secretly wrote romantic little verses to that old sea-going grandma that he lived on and loved:

> *Her skin is gray, with spots of rust,*
>
> *Her bottom's always wet.*
>
> *Contrary as a bastard cat*
>
> *She smokes a lot, and yet*
>
> *I'd never ask a finer friend.*

There would be more verses to come. As yet, Red Percifield's relations with the Galloping Ghost, as he usually thought of the *Marblehead*, were, however affectionate, still little more than those a man might have with an engaging old blue-water boarding house. Their relations had yet to be annealed by fire and battle.

For the moment he was inventorying his stock of stamps and finding that he had in the neighborhood of two hundred dollars' worth in the post office safe.

Then, just to make sure it was still all there, he took out an envelope on which he had written "Joe DeLude" and counted the money inside it. It was almost a thousand dollars which Joe had saved up while doing his tour of duty on the China Station. When Joe had first started trying to save this money, he'd kept bits of it in the tailor shop. But after these nest eggs had twice been filched in his absence, he'd asked Red to keep the money for him in the post office safe. Red was a little worried at the responsibility for so much money, had told Joe that if anything happened to it, he would, of course, be personally unable to pay it back and that, moreover, the Navy would not be responsible for it since Red had no official authorization to keep it for him.

"Why not send it to a bank in the States?" Red had asked.

"No," Joe had said, "if I got to trust somebody with my money, I'd rather it would be somebody I know. Besides, I want to have it in reach in case I need part of it."

"O.K.," Red had said, "you're the doctor. Let's just hope nothing happens to it."

Now that the money had been counted and found to be all there, Red put it back in the envelope and locked it and the stamps in the safe.

On that Sunday evening those with early morning watches to stand turned in early. It would have been difficult for a day to have been more uneventful. Tarakan lay on the Oriental side of the international date line. Back in the States it was still December 6th.

A minute or two after three that morning a plain-language message came over the radio. Ordinarily, uncoded messages are of little importance and the Junior Communications Officer, who had already been plurally dressed down for waking Malcolm McDonald, the Communications Watch Officer, in order to show him messages of no urgency whatever, hesitated for some time and then decided to take the plunge. If he caught hell for it, he caught hell. He went to McDonald's room, rapped on the door, and delivered the message.

By 3:15 the general alarm began hammering the *Marblehead*'s people into wakefulness. Hundreds of men went into action. Their reflexes had long since been conditioned to obey that alarm automatically. As their eyes opened, their feet were going toward the deck. All hands had been told there would be no more night practice calls to battle stations. Was Tarakan under attack? they wondered as they jerked on shoes. Most men were running to their stations only partially dressed, with their clothes in their hands. Over the loudspeaker system were coming the relentless words: "Man your battle stations."

When all stations had been manned, an announcement was made over the public address system: "We have just received an official plain-language message which says, 'The Japanese have commenced hostilities. Act accordingly.'" Then came the further information that the ship would get underway at dawn. And as the men went about their work, a part of their minds was struggling to encompass the huge blunt fact: "There's a war on. I'm in it." Men looked into themselves to search for signs of fear. One man wrote in his diary: "Am I afraid? Not mentally but certain reactions, nervous, perhaps, are present."

As the first glints of dawn touched the sky, the seamen on deck began to single up on the mooring lines. A few minutes later, led by the Dutch minelayer *Prinz Van Orange* whose sailors even so early in the day were wearing their quaint straw hats, the Galloping Ghost, accompanied by the destroyer Parrott and with Dutch planes overhead blinking "Good luck," stood out to sea.

Hardly, however, had she passed out of sight of Tarakan when something happened that, for the Chinese aboard, had great significance. A flying fish rose out of the water and, in its blind and hurried flight, flew through an open porthole and into the ship. Within a quarter-hour the word had flashed over the grapevine to every Chinese cook and mess attendant. Without exception they were shaking their heads in gloom. They all knew what it meant in Chinese maritime lore: bad luck, and nothing else.

THE *MARBLEHEAD* UNDERWAY IN 1935

PART 2

1

A WARSHIP IS ONLY a piece of machinery. Yet almost invariably, in the minds of the men who serve on it, it becomes a kind of governing personality. To begin with, it becomes "she," which automatically infers that her men's relationship with her shall exist principally on an emotional basis. However, psychologists say that every personality, either male or female, has certain tendencies, comprises in some degree, the characteristics of the opposite sex. So perhaps it's well to point out that as the *Marblehead* was creatively mirrored in the minds of her men, she was not entirely female, for she was somehow touched with, and became a part of, the feelings of comradeship and respect that each man felt for certain of his shipmates whom she also housed.

Moreover, she was a part of some of the most exotic memories that were in the reservoirs of the minds of her men. A little bit of Shanghai and Kobe and Rangoon and Manila had rubbed off on her, as had every seascape (and these represented many varying moods) of each of her thousands of days at sea.

Was she not the ship that had gone to the rescue of the gunboat Asheville when the latter had snapped her shaft while a typhoon raged; then got a line to her while the seas rose in mountains and the wind shrieked through the rigging? Was she not the ship that had gone boldly into Amoy when the Japs were sacking that place, and put her men ashore to protect Americans and American property? And since all this occurred after the Panay incident, hadn't Captain Robinson informed the Japanese plane-tender then in port that none of her planes were to fly over the *Marblehead*? Hadn't she laid her thin, fast-fading track across the China Sea so many times that she had come to be known, not only to her poet laureate, but to all those on the Asiatic

Station, as the Galloping Ghost of the China Coast? Memories, indeed!

Not only was the *Marblehead* associated in her men's memories with dozens of exciting adventures. It was she that had drunk their sweat and demanded their labor. By this time, she had been away from the States almost four years. Repair and upkeep facilities were usually not to be had. Her men had become, as Machinist's Mate First Class Dale Johnson phrased it, "a fix-it-yourself outfit." So, it was not the labor and ingenuity of others, but of her own men, that kept her going and in fighting trim. A part of themselves had, each day, been built into her.

Yet since in conception the *Marblehead* was predominantly female, her looks, in the minds of her men, had greatly to be considered. Well, her stacks were a little too tall, like the roof of a Model-T sedan, and too numerous. But love is not only blind; it is creative and frequently reconceives blemishes so that they become beauty marks. That her tripod foremast and bridge works were set much too far forward, and were, again, too tall and gangling to be fashionable, became a thing quickly taken for granted. But to the men on a dock securing her forward lines on a cleat well ahead of her, she was, as one looked down the hawser to her delicately wrought stem, a thing of truly feminine grace and beauty. It was much the same when one leaned against her afterdeck structure and watched her slender stern grow narrower until it vanished in the brilliant, boiling whiteness which rose, at flank speed, above her low-slung fantail.

Back among her plane catapults, afterthoughts which had been built onto her long after she'd been commissioned, some impression of modernity was created. But when one saw the heavy-muscled, sweat-shiny gunners loading her log-butted guns by hand, saw shellmen carrying 106-pound shells in their arms to the smoking breech, saw the rammerman drive home and seat the shell, one almost got the feeling of being not on the third and newest *Marblehead*, but on the first American naval vessel which had borne that name, a 507-ton steam sloop, whose guns had been mostly muzzle-loading 30-pounders. Yet before her short and belligerent career was finished, this little 158-foot ship had not only dueled Confederate forts but had captured a Confederate blockade runner, cargo and all. The second *Marblehead*, also Massachusetts built, was a somewhat more imposing vessel. She was an unarmored cruiser, 257 feet in length with a 37-foot beam and displaced 2,089 tons. Then, in 1921, just before the third and present *Marblehead* went into commission, old *Marblehead II*, which had fought honorably and well in the Spanish-American War, was put on the block and sold.

But if it were the guns of the present cruiser *Marblehead* that most called to mind her predecessors, it was perhaps her engine rooms which least resembled them. For here, in Mr. Camp's domain, where the turbines hummed their deep and powerful monotone, one became aware that this randy old girl had guts and power. Yet the ultimate secret facility which gave her the power of quick and easy seduction over her men was the indescribable ease, the almost sensuous and voluptuous grace with which her hull rode and slipped through the seas as, just now, it was doing as the ship headed south for Balikpapan, Borneo; already, unlike her forebears, in retreat on her first wartime day.

2

As the bladed stem of the *Marblehead* cut through the swells of the now hostile Celebes Sea, many of her people had a queer feeling in the pits of their stomachs. There was, to begin with, that feeling of strangeness that inhabits one who has been roused in the middle of the night with exciting news and who has not, subsequently, gone back to bed. The Japanese had taken a monumental sock at the United States Navy when it wasn't looking.

How great was the damage? How many vacant places would there be in the battle line, which one had become accustomed to thinking of and depending upon in its full might?

The news was still coming, and Ensign John Bracken, at the captain's direction, broadcast the flashes over the public address system as they arrived. His voice was now being heard throughout the ship. "The *President Harrison* has been sunk. The Japanese flag is flying over Wake. For reasons of security the damage at Pearl Harbor is not being given in detail. At least several hundred Army and Navy personnel are dead as a result of these attacks. You will be informed as more details come in."

All over the ship men were discussing this ambush. Many, as they did so, were sharpening the sheath knives which, now that an attack might occur at any time, they had taken out of their lockers and were wearing on their belts. These knives could be used, in case the ship was sinking, to cut away the lines in which a man might be fouled. Too, they'd keep a man from feeling utterly helpless when the sharks began to close in. Most of the forward repair gang had spent years on the China Station and had buddies and ex-shipmates in Manila and Pearl Harbor at the time. How many of these were now dead or maimed? There was no way of knowing.

One sailor there in forward repair told of a time when he'd had duty in China, of bumping by accident into a Japanese major who then had given him a hard push and spat some nasty Japanese talk at him.

"What'd you do?" Bull Aschenbrenner asked.

"I swatted him right in the puss. That busted his spectacles. Then I took his sword and broke it over my knee. But the Japs raised so much hell about it that the Consul got the skipper to find out who did it. I admitted it, and there was a lot more business between the Japs and the Consul and finally I had to pay four bucks for a new set of glasses."

"Should have paid ten," the Bull said, "and then gone back and broke his neck."

Topside every lookout, both surface and sky, had been ordered to keep a sharp watch for periscopes and planes.

As the sun set that evening, there was a kind of quiet sadness among many of the men as they watched its fiery rim sink below the horizon. This was their first wartime night at sea. Always before, being young, they'd had every right to expect to see that same sun the following morning. Now it was problematical. Night is the time of harvest and fruitfulness for submarines. And considerable practice is required to be able to fall asleep among them with any great degree of peacefulness and assurance. When anything has been accomplished a dozen or a hundred times, it seems that it might be done again. But this first night many men were fretful and tossed in their bunks.

Going into battle a ship's crew would have a sense of initiative and direction and focused determination. They would know that when the shooting started, they would be at their guns, on both feet, fighting. But tonight, they were full of awareness of the menace of silent ambush, of awakening too late, amid a scene of horror and hopelessness in a burning, sinking ship. And men with the topside duty, or any duty above the waterline, were glad of it.

But the night passed without alarums, and early next morning the machine gunners from their nest atop the foremast sang out that Balikpapan was now visible, lying two points off the starboard bow.

Balikpapan, though also an oiling port, was a clean, attractive town several times the size of Tarakan. Like Tarakan, it was green and tropical, only not quite so flat. Its oil installations and tanks could be seen from well out to sea. There were high mountains behind the town, but they lay well back. One got the impression that it would be impossible to walk a hundred yards into the matted jungle. It was no doubt the impenetrability of the jungle which accounted for the profusion of native boats which served not only for fishing but as the means of transport for the fishermen's families.

As the *Marblehead* slid into port her people saw that the *President Madison* was already tied up and they presumed they'd probably convoy her out of the immediate danger zone. But the two primary jobs, as soon as the tugs had brought the cruiser alongside the pier, were to fuel and strip ship. And as the hoses were brought aboard and the five-inch streams of oil started gushing into her tanks, Mr. Drury set his people to clearing the ship to fight. Soon the dock began to look like an open-air junk market of outstanding proportions. Furniture, boxes, both motorboats were put ashore, even the little pulpit at which the captain also stood when he held mast and meted out military justice, and nobody was sorry to see this symbol of retribution go.

It was found that two of the boat davits interfered with the possible trajectory of one of the 3-inch guns. These davits were huge, cast-iron affairs, and it was necessary to put a man over the side to cut away the locking jaws. The Bull was sent for; a bos'n's chair was rigged, and the Bull with his acetylene torch was slung over the side.

As the blade of eye-stinging flame ate through the huge locking jaws, the big davits plunged, with a mighty splash, into the water. The Bull, delighted by this orgy of ordered destruction, looked up and grinned at his peering shipmates just as a small boy might who, with full permission, had been throwing rocks not through windowpanes, but through plate glass windows.

But there was one little luxury which had to go that saddened everybody. It affected two people in particular: Captain Robinson and his coxswain, Shorty Horning. That was when the captain's gig was sent ashore. It had been the pride and joy of the captain, whom it had carried, and always with ebullience and jauntiness, to so many pleasant and exciting meetings on shore. Shorty, who'd certainly not been without proprietary feelings and concern, had always kept it pin-point bright, its decks varnished, and its upper works decorated with fancy canvas work, coxcombing, and cross-pointing. The look in the skipper's eye, as this gig left the ship for the last time, was one that nobody who saw it could ever forget. It was the final point of cleavage with a past that had been an extremely happy one.

Then Lt. Browning was suddenly flying across the ship and down the gangway like a frantic seagull. There had been a big chest in his room which was to have been unpacked and put ashore. But when, from the bridge, he'd seen it going ashore, it was being carried not by two men, but by four strong, sweating Chinese.

"My God," he thought, "they're going to throw it away while all my clothes are still in it!"

However, he managed to overtake the Chinese before the chest could be dumped into a garbage scow.

As the stripping of the ship proceeded, Captain Robinson went over to the *President Madison*. When he boarded her, the frightened passengers, who looked to him for protection and salvation, began to cheer as he passed along the deck.

On the following day, December 10th, an unidentified plane circled in the distance as the *S.S. Jean La Fitte* slipped into port. The *Marblehead* went to air defense, but no attack materialized. And then, a little later in the day, came profoundly disquieting news.

The power was switched on the public address system. The men heard: "I have very grave news for you. The British battleships *Repulse* and *Prince of Wales* now lie on the bottom of the China Sea. They were sunk, with great loss of life, by torpedoes launched from Japanese aircraft. The Philippines have been under severe attack by Japanese aircraft. The casualties in Pearl Harbor are now said to have neared 3,000 Army and Navy personnel. The Japanese News Agency Domei in an unconfirmed report declares that two of our battleships, the *Oklahoma* and *West Virginia*, were sunk in the Pearl Harbor attack, that four more battleships and four cruisers were heavily damaged. I repeat that this last is an unconfirmed report emanating from the enemy."

The power was switched off. Men looked at each other, stunned. Was the Japanese air arm omnipotent and omnipresent? Were men-of-war which fight on the surface obsolete? For if those great British and American battlewagons, with their vast belts of bulges designed to serve as torpedo shock absorbers, couldn't take it from the Japanese fliers, what chance had an old bucket like the *Marblehead* whose A.A. battery was but a tiny fraction of any of those capital ships and whose slender sides had no such protection?

Any torpedo that struck her would strike below her fragile armor belt which was only three inches thick at its heaviest. Her main battery could not be used against planes, and the seven 3-inch A.A.'s plus four .50 calibre machine guns atop the foremast and four more aft amounted to something considerably less than impressive. But the general feeling was: Well, that's all we've got; we're in this thing now, and we'll fight with what we have. Besides, whenever survival ceased to be logical, then the skipper would somehow work a miracle. Captain Robby, they felt, would see them through.

The news of the following afternoon was that an unidentified aircraft carrier was in the Java Sea to the south, probably for the purpose of intercepting the Allied shipping which was being collected and which warships such as the *Marblehead* would undertake to convoy out of the zone of most imminent danger. This report went to the captain. But the news that came over the loudspeaker system was the simple statement: "Germany and Italy have declared that a state of war exists between the German Reich and the Italian Empire on one hand, and the United States on the other."

Then three days later came the first of many such reports, to follow. Radio San Francisco reported that the U.S. light cruiser *Marblehead* had been sunk.

And the men aboard her, who knew she wasn't, still received little comfort as they visualized the grief and despair which were moving into hundreds of American homes, in city slums, small towns, in farmhouses in the Middle West, and on other ships at sea. They knew their families were staring at the wall, thinking of sharks and the unutterable loneliness a man feels as a foreign, hostile sea slowly encompasses him.

3

On December 14th, the day that the *Marblehead* was reported lost, she was, as a matter of fact, still in Balikpapan harbor. Shortly after noon the *Houston* and the *Boise* came into port, accompanied by the American naval auxiliary vessels *Otus*, *Holland*, and *Isabel* and four destroyers. The *Boise* had rushed out to bolster the cruiser force of the Asiatic Fleet and raise its number to three. By now the harbor was packed with ships and was so rich a prize for Japanese planes that the most rigorous scouting precautions were taken.

Meanwhile, where it was possible, men visited their buddies on other ships. Some of the visitors who came aboard the *Marblehead* on the following day had been in Cavite when it was bombed. The *Marblehead*'s people gathered round them as they told how the hospital at Canacao had been bombed to bits. The minesweeper *Bittern* had burnt to the water's edge. Of something like 200 men aboard the destroyer *Peary*, only forty had survived. Most were killed in the general mess compartment on which there was a direct hit.

It was plain by the expression on the faces of the listeners that they were drifting, in imagination, into the shattered, burning bowels of those unfortunate ships. Expressions mixed of hopelessness, melancholy and pain were on their faces. Then almost imperceptibly they'd shake off the evil dream and their jaws would set.

On the following Tuesday, in company with the old aircraft tender Langley, fleet oilers Trinity and Pecos, the supply vessel Gold Star and destroyers Preston, Paul Jones, Stewart, and Barker, the *Marblehead* left Balikpapan and again headed south, this time for Makassar harbor. The Gold Star had been on her way to Guam when hostilities broke out. She had a cargo of food, beer, and whisky, and the *Marblehead* men were naturally more interested in her welfare than in that of the other ships. As Shipfitter Bernie Wardzinski said, "They may have sneaked in and knocked off Pearl Harbor, but by God they'll never get that beer."

Warrant Officer Jarvis noted, "Men who've never given much thought to observation before now are busy scanning the sea and air for the Japs. Engineers off duty can be found acting as lookouts or asking Chief Gunner's Mate Thomas, one of the ship's crack gun captains, how to operate this or that gun, where the ammunition comes from, and other things they may need to know to help fight the ship."

Other men were taking steps to try to bring the antiquated old vessel nearer into fighting trim. She had no super-sonic equipment for spotting submerged subs. She'd have to depend on the destroyers to do that. But worst of all, she had no T.B.S., which is to say, no short-range voice radio for fast communication with the other ships of the task force. But boyish-looking Frank Blasdel, a J.G. and Mike Drury's assistant damage control officer, and Lt. Dick Hay, communications officer, were creating one out of odds and ends of gear aboard ship.

Yet while the trip to Makassar was one of tension and excitement in the minds of many of the men, it was, so far as non-imagined events went, largely lacking in excitement. A school of whales, which were first thought to be submarines, was sighted, and a floating mine which one of the escort ships destroyed by gunfire.

In order that the Gold Star could keep up, the convoy steamed along at about eight knots, which was, a few felt, far too slow and submarine-vulnerable; a speed at which to risk a cruiser. In any case the convoy reached Makassar the following Friday.

The entrance into the harbor was a tedious one due to the reefs which encircled it. Makassar itself was an old and feudal-looking town built, somebody said, back about the time when Christopher Columbus was pawning the most newsworthy jewels in Spain. The red-roofed, white buildings and the streets were clean and attractive.

The *Marblehead* picked up provisions at once and none of her officers thought she would even remain in Makassar overnight. But as the blazing hot afternoon turned into night she was still there. That evening over the radio her people heard the first Christmas carols of the season.

As one day followed another, the *Marblehead* and her convoy remained in port. There was no liberty since the ships might leave on a moment's notice. The harbor was full of little lepi-lepi boats which resembled sampans. They had rectangular sails with a mast fastening a little short of midway in the sail. Some had bright canvas streamers hanging from the sails. But though the harbor sights were bright, the men on the *Marblehead* were anything but gay as Christmas approached. The fall of Manila was already a foregone conclusion. And it was clear now that this was only the beginning. The Japanese were on the advance. The Allies had not, and knew they had not, the means to stop them. For those with the job of stemming that tide, it was clear that help would not arrive in time.

On December 16th the convoy cleared Makassar Harbor and the next day Captain Robinson noted in his line-a-day diary: "We creep southward hugging the coast of Celebes. Glad when night comes."

4

By Christmas, the convoy had reached the Dutch naval base of Surabaya, Java. Surabaya, which lay on the flat, humid Javanese coastal plain, had to be entered by a long and intricate approach through shallow and poorly marked sandbars. Dutch and native houses, on whose red roofs the sun beat down in eye-stinging brilliance, lay in clustered villages at intervals along the shore. The harbor was crowded with ships of all nations as well as picturesque native craft.

Christmas, while the *Marblehead* lay in the Netherlands Royal Navy Yard, was just another day. No gifts, no nothing, except that shipmates said "Merry Christmas" to each other. Too, there was turkey with the traditional accessories. And as the men ate, Captain Robinson walked among the mess tables and said, "Merry Christmas, men."

So much was implicit in those three words. It was a terrible Christmas, not merry at all, and the future was black. Yet here was the skipper doing the only thing he could, saying the only thing he could to let them know that, since it was in fact a dreadful Christmas, he did deeply wish it might have been a better and merrier one. But also implicit in those three words and this little gesture, was the further fact that he thought of them not merely as instruments for the effective operation of the ship, but as his shipmates whom he respected, had faith in, and liked.

As he left, one man, whose eyes were growing a little moist, expressed the sentiments of the rest when he said, "There's a man you'd follow to hell and back." How accurately prophetic that statement was nobody knew at the time.

As for the captain, once he'd made his rounds and, as it were, paid his respects to the crew, he began thinking of his wife.

Mrs. Robinson, before she had married the skipper, had been an actress. He thought now of her delicate sense of situation. Long before the war began, she had feared and dreaded the time when it would come. As he had left on this cruise, she had known that war might start before she saw him again, that he and his ship would be in the forefront of the fight, and she might be saying goodbye for the last time. But as they parted, she'd mentioned none of her fears and premonitions, had simply smiled and said, "Have a good time, Robby. But take it easy on the curves;" a pleasantry when seriousness could have accomplished nothing. How wonderful it would be if today he could talk to her over radio telephone and say, "Merry Christmas and don't worry."

He had decided that Japs or no Japs a part of the crew should be allowed some Christmas liberty. When the men went ashore, they listened to a band playing Christmas music. They thought of their families, what they would be doing today, of all the thousands of miles that separated them from home.

Bull Aschenbrenner, as he mopped his broad, sweating brow, would have bet you that the snow was at least a foot thick in New Ulm, Minnesota, that the kids were all out sliding on Christmas sleds, and skating along the Minnesota River on six-hour-old skates. His grandmother would have cooked a turkey that morning that she'd stuffed the night before, or maybe a goose.

He knew the kinfolk would all be there and that some of them would say, "Well, where do you suppose Shinny is today?" And he thought of his grandmother not knowing and being worried, and he thought, "Christ, if I could only do something to get this God-damned war over with so she wouldn't worry anymore."

Everywhere men were thinking about home. The Deacon, the hotshellman, said, "Christ died that there might be peace on earth. Now look what these Japs have gone and done. It ain't right. " And he meant it and was opposed to it in every fiber.

This day men lived through thousands of old scenes: a cow's misty breath in a cold barn at milking time, the fellows who used to hang around the pool hall, Nancy Bevins' thigh, the garage at quitting time when men washed their hands with Lava soap and thought, "Another day, another dollar," Roseland, the World's Fair, a dime in the toe of a black cotton stocking.

Most of the officers went to the Simpang Club, a delightful place, spacious with verandas and snow-white tables and cool wicker chairs, where the maître d'hôtel spoke English and where, besides marvelous Heineken's beer, there was rice taffel, a kind of wet curry to which was added, as the successive waiters arrived, an astonishingly manifold assortment of meats and tropical vegetables and spiced fruits, and which, in one of its lesser manifestations, was listed on the menu by the remarkable name of Nazigoring.

Dr. Wildebush spent the afternoon buying an extraordinarily expensive and potent radio, and Van Bergen and Zern went for a drive inland across the ten-mile plain, which lay behind the Dutch naval base and which was dotted with rice paddies and groves of flowering trees. They drove on up the steep mountains to the little resort on top where the air, in contrast to the steaming heat of the plains, was almost uncomfortably cool to men in white shirts and uniform shorts. All the houses had spectacular flower gardens and swimming pools where the bright sun danced on blue-green water.

On the way back Van Bergen inquired of the driver, "Whatse callem flower tree?"

The driver turned, saw he was being addressed, did his best to comprehend the question, and said, "At the moment, sir, the botanical name escapes me... Would the native word suffice?"

Van Bergen said it would, and he and Zern went on back to the ship.

Some of the men went to the Orange Hotel, others to Hollendorn restaurant to try to catch up on their consumption of such items as fresh tomatoes, tenderloin steak and Dutch beer.

Fire Controlman First Class Riches discovered a fortuneteller in a Marine canteen and, impressed by the things the fortuneteller told him of his past, invited several of his comrades to come along and have their fortunes told too. Among these was Shipfitter Bernie Wardzinski, whom everybody called "Ski" for short. Ski went along but refused to have his fortune told. He was an easy-going fellow, well-liked by his shipmates, and a friend of the Bull's. Ski was as dark as the Bull was blond and stood some five and a half feet tall. Ordinarily Ski was agreeable to almost any kind of excursion ashore, but today he was being stubborn about the fortuneteller.

"Come on, Ski," Riches urged. "This guy is really good. He'll tell about your past first and then about your future."

"I didn't say he wasn't good," Ski said. "I just said I ain't going to have my fortune told."

"But don't you want to know what's going to happen to you?"

"I already know."

"The hell you do! What?"

"It ain't good and I don't want to hear him say it."

"Why ain't it good?"

By now the color had left Ski's face. "I'm going to die ... soon ..." Ski said. "I don't want to. I'm afraid of dying ... but I'm going to die, and I know it... I don't need this guy to ... to rub it in."

There was a silence. Riches was convinced and frightened. But after a moment he said, "Aw, snap out of it, Ski. It's just something you ate. You other guys go on in. Me and Ski'll go knock off a beer."

To the men who did have their fortunes told, the man said, "Soon all of you will be in a great battle, in which many will be killed."

Metalsmith Moran, the boxer with the glass hands, and Dale Johnson, Machinist's Mate, went souvenir hunting. They wanted to get a few trinkets to send home. Dale Johnson was married, loved his wife very much, and felt a present from the Dutch East Indies would please her. It was not, however, until they got back to the ship that they found that each curio bore a tiny sticker on which, in blue ink, was printed, "Made in U.S.A."

This was not true of the curio which Chief Water Tender Bridges had bought. He stopped to watch a snake charmer and had become so fascinated that he had bought one of the fakir's snakes, in order that he might perform with it personally for the entertainment of his shipmates. What the outcome of such a performance might have been was, however, never learned, since Bridges had a disagreement with a rickshaw man on the way back to the ship and began chasing him with the wriggling cobra which, no doubt to the benefit of all, escaped in the melee.

Others of the crew, in their loneliness, proceeded to get thoroughly soused on Bols gin out of stone bottles. Liberty expired at nine-thirty that night and they were still not back at the ship. Then when the Shore Patrol rounded them up, they knew they were in for it. They would be put on report; their permanent record would have a black mark on it. Already they could hear Commander Goggins' biting questions as he had them up to the preliminary mast where the executive officer decides whether any of the men have a good excuse for their misdemeanors or whether they must stand trial before the captain. They could hear the commander asking them if they did not know that their country was at war and that all misconduct under such circumstances becomes much more serious and reprehensible. Suppose the ship had sailed and they had not been aboard? The charge would then have been desertion, the result a good many years in Portsmouth naval prison. Either that or be shot. Well, it was going to be tough, all right, but there was nothing to do now but face the music, accept the fine and the extra duty. A hell of a Christmas.

As the miscreants came aboard, John Bracken was junior officer of the deck. He asked the meaning of this tardiness. Heads ducked. "We got drunk, sir."

Ensign Bracken looked them over carefully. Their clothes were rumpled and dirty and torn. They were pretty much the worse for wear. A few were weaving on their feet. Gloom and guilt hung about them as thickly as the cloud formations around Diamond Head in Hawaii.

"This has been a lousy Christmas," Ensign Bracken said. "None of us have gotten any gifts. But I'm going to give you one. Go sleep it off with a happy heart. Nobody's name goes on report."

Heads raised. Eyes stared in disbelief and wonderment. The reason they did not kiss Ensign Bracken was because that method of expressing gratitude is frowned upon in the United States Navy.

But there had been two celebrators who had not required this Yule-time dispensation. For as the minute hand had drawn almost within touching distance of the time when liberty would expire, a taxi had come roaring down the docks. Brakes were slammed on as it drew up to the gangway, broadside-to, and two men had leaped out. One was carrying his jumper and neckerchief in his hand; the other wore only shoes, drawers, and his white hat; the rest trailed from his arms as the two of them ran up the gangway. They saluted the officer of the deck, grinned in happy triumph and, certain that the officer must applaud this violent effort and be pleased with their success, said, "Well, sir, we made it. Didn't we?"

USS *BOISE* (JULY 1938)

5

New Year's Eve found the *Marblehead* and her convoy off the northeastern tip of Timor en route for Darwin. A couple of ships had reported sighting submarines, but nothing came of these possible contacts. There was a distress call from the minesweeper *Heron*: "Am being attacked." But she was 300 miles away, and the *Marblehead* could not abandon her own convoy to go to the *Heron*'s assistance. And, without looking up the data in *Jane's*, the old hands knew that, to defend herself, the *Heron* had exactly two 3-inch guns and a few machine guns. She was, by now, in all probability sinking.

The officers in the wardroom at lunch that day were sorry they could not have gone to help the *Heron*, whose people many of them knew personally. But since it was impossible for one ship to be two places at once, the officers became resigned, and the conversation general.

The *Marblehead*'s wardroom, which stretched from side to side of the ship on the main deck just under the after part of the bridge works, had three dining tables running fore and aft, leather couches, and a circular library table on each side of the dining tables. The Chinese mess boys kept it immaculate and, unlike some insufferable mess boys on other ships, never replenished the coffee in the silex coffeemakers by simply adding fresh coffee to the last remaining tar-like inch of the old. Here there was a radio, a few old books and magazines, and a place to talk. Generally speaking, rank at the dining tables read from fore to aft and from port to starboard, with Commander Goggins sitting at the forward end of the port-most table since Captain Robinson traditionally dined alone in his own quarters.

Frequently the conversation lagged. Men at sea in wartime on fighting ships are almost always sleepy. Though a man's watches are four hours on and eight hours off, the off eight hours often seem entirely filled with General Quarters, inspections, reports, meals, unforeseen difficulties with equipment, so that four or five, at the outside six, hours' sleep in twenty-four is the most that anyone usually gets.

But just as there were bull sessions and occasional extracurricular crap games below decks, sometimes, both in the evening and during casual hours of the day, there were long discussions of hundreds of things in the wardroom: Japanese technical advancements. Their reputed inferiority in fire control. Dinner at Carvel Hall at Annapolis in the early spring when shad were running in the Potomac. The spacious, school-townishly-sleepy dining room with the flat-footed Negro waiters. The moonlight strained through the trees outside. Slightly drooling recollections of the Welsh rabbit at Tom's Dixie Kitchen in Manila. Or perhaps nostalgic discussions of Shanghai's elegant ladies of the evening who were, as a matter of fact, at their most elegant in the afternoon when they drove in victorias along Bubbling Well Road holding lacy Flora Dora parasols over their heads, themselves dressed to the nines, and with footmen on the box.

It was pleasant to remember how, after these airings, the girls would return to the drawing-room floor of the houses and entertain callers in any of a number of discreet private reception rooms with tea, small cakes and conversation—none of the more intimate inclinations of their gentlemen clients being catered to until the evening. There were also, of course, in Shanghai, many less distinguished and more gymnastic bordellos on Blood Alley, joints such as Short-time Annie's, where on Friday nights the girls danced in bras and panties. But this was hardly the sort of place one admitted knowing too much about in wardroom conversations.

Discussions of science were strictly no holds barred. But religion was usually handled lightly and with reasonable consideration. And a large part of the time it was Mr. Camp, the engineering officer, who started the ball rolling, taking any viewpoint he felt would be provocative and lead to interesting discussion, pretending to defend what he didn't at all believe. That failing, he purposely pretended to be an authority, to some degree, on matters of which he knew virtually nothing in order to start the conversational chase, the object of which would be to bring him to bay. But his subtle and elegant elusive tactics almost always served to extricate him from the most seemingly inextricable discursive cul-de-sac.

Rain fell in torrents all New Year's Eve and most of the day. Then when it stopped, some of the junior officers moved chairs out on the cigarette deck where the air was a few degrees cooler than that inside the ship, but Commander Goggins decided that the presence of those chairs would reduce the efficiency of the ship if she were suddenly attacked, and ordered the chairs removed.

But it was only a short distance to Darwin, Australia, and the fact that a submarine was reported to be lurking at the mouth of the harbor took the young officers' attention off the matter of the chairs on the cigarette deck.

The ships reached port in safety, however, and all the men who had expected Port Darwin to offer anything in the way of excitement and entertainment took one look and knew the worst. Though it was to be the base for the Army and Navy and headquarters for the Air Force in the Far East, it was a bleak, barren town about three blocks long and two blocks wide. It was a typical frontier town with buildings made of corrugated iron, almost none of which were more than one story high, and the windows were boarded up because the owners were tired of replacing panes which drunks had smashed by throwing beer bottles through them.

What's more, the rainy season was on. Red Percifield noted, "It rains so hard the native fishermen dip the rainwater off the top of the ocean and drink it." The town was a sea of red mud. As Captain Robinson viewed this depressing sight from the ship's bridge, he said to Commander Goggins, "Look at this God-forsaken place. It hasn't one redeeming feature."

"Oh, yes, it has, sir," Commander Goggins said. "There isn't a God-damned palm tree in sight!"

But the men who hated Darwin most of all were the *Marblehead*'s communications people. Because hardly had they arrived when they learned that the local shore station was hopelessly unable to handle the communications traffic piled on it. So, the *Marblehead* became "Radio

Darwin" and for about three days almost every communication in the Asiatic Station cleared through her. She had no additional assistance whatever. And to make it harder, all the Army messages came through her too and each of these had to be encoded before sending. For the officers, this extra work was somewhat mitigated by the fact that all of them were made honorary members of H.M.A.S. Melville, the officers' club, where a man could at least know the consolation of a few cold beers.

The *Marblehead* enlisted men caused something of a stir in Darwin's humble restaurants. It was not so much the brave quantities of beer they drank that caused remark, as the habit many of the men had of ordering a steak dinner for their main course and a second such dinner for dessert.

But, as in the case of other men who've worn bell-bottomed trousers and a coat of Navy blue, the refreshment consumed was not limited to such pacific items as steak and beer. Three fellows, all good friends, very tough and pleasant engineers, came under the influence of more violent potions, and, at one point in the proceedings, two of them arrived at the decision that the third was an iniquitous fellow. And, realizing that it is the duty of all right-thinking people to punish iniquity and, where possible, to wipe it out, they turned-to to beat up their erring colleague, an undertaking which they accomplished with noteworthy success. By the time they had finished, he was bleeding satisfactorily in a number of places; one eye was entirely closed, and the very sag of his knees bore testimony to the fact that he had just undergone a fairly rigorous experience.

"Well and good," decided his chastisers. Evil had been adequately demonstrated against if, that was, the bounds of friendship were not to be overstepped. So, they gathered up their confrere and took him back to the ship. As far as they were concerned, all was forgiven.

But by the time they reached the ship, their battered comrade had begun to recover a little and, furthermore, to feel imposed upon. So as the three passed through the first watertight door, the man with the hurt feelings took hold of a dog wrench, a foot-long length of one-inch iron pipe that is slipped over dog ends to give greater leverage in tightening doors and hatches. With this instrument, he took aim on the nearest of his recent assailants and let drive, laying open his head, and, in short order, meting out exactly the same treatment to the other one.

This mayhem had not been accomplished without some clatter, and by now the makings of a riot were at hand. But before sides could properly be chosen, and enough dog wrenches and hose nozzles gathered, Edmundson, Chief Master-at-Arms, got there, retired for reinforcements and then scattered the crowd. The three militant friends were carried down to sickbay where Dr. Ryan, annoyed at having his holiday evening spoiled and further irritated at the threats now being yammered back and forth among the combatants, set about sewing these hearties up without benefit of anesthesia of any sort.

As he stitched up one man's head, another was telling of the further demolition he had in mind for the patient. Suddenly the threatener discovered he was out of cigarettes, was given one by his former assailant, only to snatch it out of his hand and bark, "Thank ye, ye bastard." Which, of course, was the last that was heard of this friendly tiff and perhaps over-emphatic expression of a temporary difference in viewpoint.

When the *Marblehead* cleared Darwin in company with the *Boise* and a Dutch merchantman carrying American troops and supplies, she was headed for Surabaya, and pelting along at fifteen knots. One young officer noted: "As the war progresses, most of us [that is, the junior officers] are getting over our initial reluctance about sleeping below. Either it's the fact that you don't care, or that initial fear has been dissipated. I must admit I was leery myself about sleeping down there. I took my radio back down today, though." He did not mention the enormous safety factor which accrues to a ship that has lifted her speed from eight to fifteen knots.

Down in the enlisted men's quarters there was a pleasant reunion. The *Marblehead* had received a small draft of new men aboard at Darwin. One of those men had been Yeoman First Class Beauford Gabriel. For Beauford Gabriel, now at work in the ship's Executive Office, his transfer to the *Marblehead* amounted to the fulfilment of an aspiration of long standing. He had previously served on the *Lexington*, had liked her fine and been proud of his connection with her. But he had wanted to transfer to the *Marblehead* because his brother Ralph was a ship's cook aboard her. Also aboard was Dave Hodges, storekeeper second class, who was from Redlands, California, the Gabriels' hometown. These lads had all been old pals since the days when the three of them had got up at five o'clock every morning to go down to the office of the Redlands Facts to get their papers and start their delivery. Each of them now, as they were rejoined, had different clippings from the Facts that had been sent out to them, and among the three of them they could reconstruct a good part of what had been going on back home.

Ralph and Dave were particularly amused by a postcard Beauford had. On the top was a picture of a sleeping sailor; beneath the picture was printed:

A Sailor's Prayer

Now I lay me down to sleep,

I pray the Lord my Soul to keep.

Grant no other sailor take

My shoes and socks before I wake.

Lord guard me in my slumber

And keep my hammock on its number.

May no clues nor lashings break

And let me down before I wake.

Keep me safely in Thy sight

And grant no fire drill tonight.

And in the morning let me wake

Breathing scents of sirloin steak.

God protect me in my dreams

And make this better than it seems.

Grant the time may swiftly fly

When I shall rest on high

In a snowy feather bed

Where I long to rest my head

Far away from all these scenes

And the smell of half-done beans.

Take me back into the land

Where they don't scrub down with sand,

Where no demon Typhoon blows,

Where the women wash the clothes.

God, thou knowest all my woes,

Feed me in my dying throes.

Take me back. I'll promise then

Never to leave Home again...

Four Years Later

Our Father who art in Washington,

Please, dear Father, let me stay,

Do not drive me now away.

Wipe away my scalding tears

And let me stay for Thirty Years.

Please forgive me all my past

And things that happened at the mast.

Do not my request refuse

And let me stay another cruise.

And though all three of these men might, at some distant date, be longing to go on another cruise, they would at the moment have loved to set eyes on Redlands, California, and, that failing, at least on a month-old issue of its newspaper. But in any case, Beauford was relieved to be aboard the same ship with his younger brother. Now, if Ralph needed any looking after, he'd get it.

In this same draft was another young man who, when asked by a burly petty officer if he were ready to face certain gorily described terrors of combat, had given the straightforward reply, "Well, I certainly didn't come out here just to be a gold star in my mother's window."

6

As the ships ran along the route to Surabaya, they were ready to fight as a team. Since the Senior Officer and OTC (Officer in Tactical Command) was on the *Boise*, she gave the orders for the task force. And as the ships steamed on, the men aboard the *Marblehead* were a little jealous of the *Boise*'s sleeker, better lines and the fact that she was, hands down, the best ship and, all things being equal, could kill the *Marblehead* quick in a fight.

They were both light cruisers, which is to say they were armed with six instead of eight-inch guns. But where the *Marblehead* weighed in at 7,050 tons, the *Boise* was a 10,000-ton vessel and thirteen years younger. The *Boise's* 600-foot hull was fifty feet longer and had ten feet more beam. Only in speed did the *Marblehead* have her bested. While the *Marblehead's* power plant generated only 90,000 horsepower, her four screws could drive her at thirty-five knots, which was two and a half knots faster than the 100,000-horsepower plant of the *Boise* could drive her longer, broader hull. But in guns there was no comparison. The *Boise* had an antiaircraft battery of eight 5-inch guns plus smaller ones. And where the old *Marblehead* had a main battery of ten 6-inch guns, the *Boise* had fifteen, and when she let go from all turrets in rapid fire at night, she gave the impression of being totally afire. It was only natural then, that the commander of such a cruiser, which was a match for any light cruiser that fought on the seas, should be senior to the commander of such a semi-obsolescent country cousin as the *Marblehead*.

Since no Japanese ships were met, the principal item of interest aboard the *Marblehead*, as is so often the case with communities ashore, was a trial.

A seaman was accused of disobedience to orders, abusive language, and striking a petty officer. Captain Robinson had said the accused must be tried before a summary court. Lt. Frank Blasdel was counsel for the defense, Ensign Bracken the prosecutor. The accused pleaded not guilty, but Ensign Bracken set out to prove that the accused was and had been a bad actor in general who went about threatening his way instead of working. But when the trial had dragged on for three days, he lost patience with the bumbling of the usually efficient court reporter, John Wohlschlaeger, and, while the court was in recess, delivered himself of the opinion that Frank Blasdel was a good kid, but, legally speaking, was unable to distinguish between his own backside and Mount Vesuvius. The trial went on, however, until Friday, when the ship, on orders from the *Boise* had detached herself and gone into Koepang Bay, on Timor, to refuel from the *Trinity*. By this time the court had acted. The accused was found guilty of two charges, got thirty days in the brig on bread and water and was fined $164.

There was, however, a story behind the procedure at this trial about which Ensign Bracken knew nothing. And that had to do with the wandering attention of John Wohlschlaeger, ordinarily the captain's yeoman, who was acting as the court reporter at the trial.

John Wohlschlaeger was in love. It was not with any living, breathing girl that he'd ever seen that he was in love, but with a little pile of letters and a photograph. He had hoped to find a few more letters at Darwin. But the ship had received no mail whatever, and he was disconsolate.

There really was a girl back in New England who was represented by the little pile of letters and the photograph, but John had never seen her. She was, as a matter of fact, Joe DeLude's little sister.

Wohlschlaeger's interest in her had all come about much earlier when he'd seen her picture one day in the tailor shop. Joe had enjoyed talking about her so much, and himself saw her with so much affection, that John had said, "Well, we been shipmates for a long time, Joe, and she seems like a mighty sweet girl. How about giving me a tumble to her by letter? When you write to her, just tell her that John Paul Jones never had anything that I haven't got, and I'll write a letter to go with yours."

Joe thought that over and decided John would be a nice fellow for his sister to know. Both men wrote letters and sent them off together, and when Joe's sister had answered Joe's letter, she'd also answered John's, and thereafter whenever there was mail call and the ship's company stormed down upon and engulfed the tiny post office, John was always No. 2 in line.

Oddly enough, the man who was always No. 1 was a man who had never received but one letter in two years. But whenever mail call was sounded, he was always there, No. 1 in line, full of hope and belief. Then when there'd be no mail for him, he'd walk away sadly in real and heartbroken surprise.

Then John would bounce up to the window and say:

"O.K., Red, deal me out about a half a dozen letters from you-know-who, and also give me some mail for Joe."

John was almost as interested in Joe's getting mail as he was in getting it himself. John would read his own letters on the way to the tailor shop to deliver Joe's, so that as Joe finished page one of his first letter, he'd be there to seize it and devour it.

After that John would go to his bunk, reread his own letters, and start answering them, not en masse, but one at a time, letter for letter, telling her every place he'd been, things he'd seen or thought, and give accurate descriptions of whatever curios or pieces of Oriental linen Joe had added to his collection.

Then there'd be nothing more to do but dream until the next mail call and wonder how she actually was in person.

Sunday, January 11th, was a beautiful bright day in Koepang Bay, and everybody hoped the war would, at least for twelve or so hours, keep out of their hair so there could be liberty, and perhaps a walk in the wooded hills that surrounded the bay. But by nine o'clock a message came ordering the ship to rendezvous with other American vessels at sea, so the *Marblehead* set off at twenty knots through the dreamlike beauty of this day, slicing through a flat, blue and white, breeze-rippled sea.

Soon after the ship got underway, the Deacon opened one of the ready racks where 3-inch shells were kept, lifted the canvas, took out his Bible, leaned against the side of the splinter shield and began to read. What he was reading was only begats, but the words were holy words and the calm repetition of sentence form had a peaceful and sedative effect, which, upholstered by the loveliness of the surrounding seascape and the luxurious motion of the ship, made him quietly happy. This spell was suddenly shattered by the voice of one of the trainers declaring in loud and emphatic tones that one of the Chinese boys was a lantern-jawed son of a bitch who had emanated from an athwartships vagina and that Fook Liang was not only his name but the trainer's sentiments.

The Deacon put down his Bible, looked with uncompromising disapproval at the trainer and said, "This is Sunday. You know that ain't no way to talk."

A look of disgust spread over the trainer's face. "Look, Deacon," he said. "This is the Navy. Why didn't you hire out as a priest in the first place? You're O.K., kid, but just in the wrong racket."

The Deacon closed his Bible and said, "I wonder sometimes if there's such a lot of difference."

"You mean between the Church and the Navy! Go—*wan*. What is this?"

The Deacon's gaze turned to the azure ribbons of sea slipping past the ship's sides.

"Take a monastery," he said. "Somewhere off up in the mountains. And a Navy ship at sea. What goes on in either one? Work. Celibacy. Study and—look at the guys at every gun—contemplation. You live close to nature and you're isolated from civilization. In both cases you got strict law and discipline. Every fellow's got a job to do and he does it. But that ain't all. They both got tradition and ritual. Pipe the Admiral over the side. Each man salute the quarter deck. Give honors to passing men-of-war. Greet the dawn from behind a gun. Then muster on stations. Swab down. Everything godly and spick and span. Fight for the right, humbly, earnestly, and with real self-sacrifice. Fellows both places wear uniforms, only one is black and the other blue. Both are retreats for troubled, mixed-up spirits... Think how you feel after we been in port a few days. You're broke and got the headache and afraid you got the clapp. You've raised hell on shore and maybe broke up some stuff and you wish the ship would go on and sail before the cops come down to the pier and commence talking to Commander Goggins. Well, finally, we get the word. 'All special sea details man your stations.' You commence to single up the lines. The tugs work her out into the stream and then—well, take right now—you feel a kind of peacefulness come over you—you're back where everything is simple and you understand your job and your life. In a monastery they call it the peace of God. Why ain't it the same thing here?"

That was the Deacon's sermon for Sunday, January 11th, delivered to five other seamen at a 3-inch gun.

Later that evening one of the junior officers wrote: "Just before and during sunset we passed through Alor Strait. Perhaps it was the time of day or the changed weather, but it was the most beautiful scene I have ever witnessed. Here was a winding cut heading roughly to the north east. On our left was the island of Lomblem, while on our right was Rusa and Pandai. At some spots it was less than five miles across. The sun set behind Lomblem, making a fine lace of the trees which lined its mountains. A lot of small islands floated around like lily pads. The sea itself was as calm as glass and reflected the red-tinted clouds and hills. A little earlier we had passed by an active volcano. It was like an inverted cone inside another cone. It was smoldering but we saw no fire. After the sunset, Venus came up and was almost as bright as the moon might be. The evening was calm and peaceful: hard to realize that a war is going on."

He did not say that he expected this serenity to last. Yet for two more days it did. January 13th found the *Marblehead* in large and gorgeous Saleh Bay on Soembawa Island, surrounded by the green and purple hills, the clear blue water alive with exotic fishes. That night the ship lay at anchor and there was a glorious break in the routine: movies. They were shown several times so that the men of various watches could know the luxury of abandoning the doubtful, trying present for an hour or two. And the release was the more real in that the picture was so old that it carried its spectators back to the innocent days of prohibition and gangsterism, high-topped touring cars, and short skirts with low waistbands. So complete was the illusion, and so hungrily was it accepted, that it carried over, remained more or less intact, even while the operator changed the reel. The Mickey Mouse was fine, and there was besides a newsreel showing one of President Roosevelt's inaugurations.

Then on the morning of January 15th came two messages of a less dreamy and nostalgic and peaceful tone. The first stated that there was a concentration of Japanese shipping off Celebes, and that a light cruiser would be nominated to go up and attack. There were two light cruisers available. Then the second message came. It nominated the *Marblehead*.

ADMIRAL THOMAS HART

PART 3

1

ON JANUARY 15TH, THE native fisherman in Saleh Bay, looking up from their little boats at the towering naval vessels there, were very apt to get a false impression of the might of the American Asiatic Fleet. Had the heavy cruiser *Houston* been in port, the sight would have been even more impressive: three spanking cruisers spoiling for a fight, to say nothing of the string of destroyers nesting side by side. But all naval strength is real only in relation to that of the enemy, and had these same fishermen known that the Japanese Navy was in possession of ten times as many cruisers which could have been unleashed upon this little group, they might have been less impressed.

Even so, being human, they would still have been excited by the sight. For there is something about a cruiser, in time of war, that sets the human mind in a turmoil of wondering and imagining what's going on inside. For one can sense the brimming power of her engines and know that men must be tending them, that other men are washing clothes, typing, cooking (what?), decoding messages (again, what?), drying out signal flags. There is something secret and potent about her, like a fraternity to which one doesn't belong. It is almost impossible to look upon her and think of her merely as an engine of frightfulness, which is her aim and end.

Had these fishermen's eyes not fallen in love with the box-butted *Boise*, which now carried Admiral Glassford's flag, had they been particularly curious regarding the unattractive duckling nestling nearby, and could they have looked through the bulkheads of Captain Robinson's cabin, they would have seen the captain in session with his department heads and his executive officer, Commander Goggins, whom, though he sometimes irritated the junior officers by his perfectionism, not one of them had ever for one second doubted and failed to lean on.

Captain Robinson was sitting in a swivel chair with his back against his desk. Commander Goggins sat in a leather-upholstered chair, the others on the couch and in straight chairs.

Captain Robinson looked at his officers. Even if it had not been his way to like people, he would have liked them. They were the men who would handle his ship in circumstances that would call for the highest ability and resolution. They were good officers, would fight his ship well.

Captain Robinson smiled. "Gentlemen," he said, "I have a piece of news for you. There is a Japanese concentration at northeast Celebes. This force consists of two cruisers, one light, one heavy: ten or so destroyers, and twenty transports. We, in company with four destroyers, *the Ford, the Pope, the Parrott,* and *Bulmer,* have been delegated to attack this force.

"But this mission, while no tea party, is only the opening gun in a much bigger battle. Right now, we're a large chunk of what we've got in this area. We've got to make it count, regardless of losses. Our prestige in this part of the world will depend largely on the show we're able to put up. That's the psychological side. For the rest, we've got to do as much damage in attrition as possible to the enemy. And keep on doing it until other things in the making are in sight."

He paused and watched their faces.

He had delivered this speech as if he had been informing a basketball team of its next week's schedule. On the face of his First Lieutenant, M. J. Drury, there was no change of expression whatever. He was receiving information attentively, carefully recording each fact so that he might act upon it capably. There was also no change in Van Bergen's expression, but a slow fire was smoldering in his eyes, and entirely without knowing it, he had leaned two inches forward in his chair. The Chief Engineer, Lt. Commander Camp, was waiting to hear the rest of the story. Dr. Wildebush's mind was on tannic acid.

Captain Robinson continued. "It is, as a child could see, an extremely dangerous mission. But if we fall upon the enemy by complete surprise, we should be able to create considerable damage, and, perhaps, get away, at least from the surface ships. Whatever enemy ships come out to overhaul and sink us will be led directly across the sights of American submarines. It is even possible that the *Houston* will be somewhere in the near distance to cover our retirement. The enemy will, of course, control the sky, but, after all, we have our A. A. batteries, and if we use them well enough, we should get away."

His confidence and seriousness left nothing to be wanted.

"When this mission was first ordered," the captain went on, "it was requested that a light cruiser be nominated from the task force. Knowing the two ships available, I believe you will all agree that we were the logical choice." Not mentioning the fact that the *Marblehead* was obviously the more expendable, he said, "For while the *Boise*, with her superior fire power might create greater destruction, she is, as you know, due to the conventional manner of her gun locations, either a broadside or a fore-and-aft fighter. We, having our guns mounted much after the manner in which a porcupine mounts his quills, are not. We can, and when we charge into that Jap concentration I mean to, throw steel from every quarter. That, I consider, reason enough for our entrustment with this job. But there remains another. We are determined to do our duty. Yet none of us wishes to die. And while our chances of accomplishment lie in the distribution of our guns over the ship, our chance of survival lies in the fact that where the *Boise* has not, we do have a speed superiority of two knots over any cruiser in the Japanese fleet, and one knot over 95% of their destroyers.

"Now, gentlemen, if we undertake this attack with smartness and character, if the surprise is complete, our shooting superlative, and our luck working ... well, I think we will have a right to be a proud ship."

A tissue-paper-thin little coating of ice had come over these officers' nerve ends.

Again, Captain Robinson smiled, then asked, "Any questions?"

Commander Van Bergen spoke up. "The destroyers will illuminate the enemy?"

"Yes. Quite late and close aboard."

Captain Robinson went on to explain the tactics to be used. The anchorage where the enemy concentration lay was sheltered only on three sides. To seaward the anchorage was open. Just to the rear of the southern end of the anchorage and inland lay a mountain that, as its bulk blotted out the stars, would serve as a landmark.

But, more important, the enemy ships lay at anchor just inland off the abrupt edge of a ten-fathom shelf of sea floor which made an undersea trail that would lead the striking force, pelting along at flank speed, to the target. And since the *Marblehead* had a more dependable fathometer than the destroyers, she would lead the attack, navigating principally by her fathometer and the soundings on her charts. The destroyers would follow, in column, a little on her port quarter and using her as guide.

As the attack opened, the destroyers, with torpedo tubes already trained out, would fall upon the Japanese cruisers with a torpedo attack, while the *Marblehead*, firing, as the captain had just said, from every quarter, would engage all of the enemy destroyers which would, it was hoped, by then be in a state of confusion. As soon as torpedoes had been gotten into the enemy cruisers, the striking force destroyers, already in full momentum, were to turn upon such enemy destroyers as the *Marblehead* had not engaged and begin hammering them with gunfire. And of course, once the Japanese warships had been dealt with, the troopships would be at the Americans' mercy which, this night, would be in total abeyance.

"Are there any further questions?" the captain asked.

Had Dr. Wildebush thought that by asking a question he could have solved the futile problem of how best to treat the wounded on a sinking ship, he would have inquired.

There were no more questions.

Captain Robinson stood up.

"That will be all, gentlemen. Good luck to all of us."

Early the next day the old four-piper cruiser and the four little thousand-ton World War I destroyers, all of them her senior, but full of the physically tough romanticists that destroyer duty invariably attracts, slid out to sea, the utterly dedicated and supremely dangerous enemies of Goliath.

2

Not until the little and, technically, decrepit striking force was at sea was the word passed among the crew regarding the job ahead. The enthusiasm was terrific. The *Marblehead*'s men were strong, healthy, sentimental, curious. There was a war on. It was new. They were in it. War had long been publicized as fare only for the strongest spirits. Bring it on. The men of the *Marblehead* were being acted upon by their American heritage, their upbringing in the land of the long pass in the fourth quarter, of derring-do, of a tough fight where you get both ears cauliflowered but your name in the morning papers. Nick Carter, Davy Crockett, Dick Tracy, and John Paul Jones would have loved this scrap. The British might have done it differently. And who's to say what the French would have done? But the *Marblehead* and those four little four-pipers were making an end run with no interference. If the import and consequences were a thousand times more serious, the emotions, at this stage of the game, were much the same.

A numbness to normal values comes over yet unblooded men at war. Some were keyed so high that whether they died or conquered had become only a kind of academic symbol of who won or lost the game. That they might be maimed and live fifty more years became a matter for subsequent consideration. They had a battle to fight. Logic from every standpoint said fight ferociously and well, forget everything except the crucial present. Tingles came in the bottoms of men's feet. Jokes became frequent and brittle, not funny, but most people laughed. It was a time of the highest awareness on the most superficially mechanical plane and yet there came into being a very narrow-stemmed, lucid, and direct pipeline to the past.

Red Percifield noted, "All day we have been heading toward the spot. The afternoon was spent making plans. We have a fair picture of how things stand. But with any degree of luck we can hurt this Jap force plenty. We in forward control talked all afternoon, foolishly at times, to keep from getting nervous. This is our first action and naturally we are a bit taut. But as afternoon faded into twilight this talk died down and, in its stead, came thoughts of things in the past. I had wanted to get married before I came to China. We were serious from the start. Then I got in the Navy and she wasn't sure, but for me she is still the only one. I can almost see her now..."

As the comforting daylight faded, and very possibly for the last time, the ship began to be inhabited by women. Women in evening gowns, others in cozy wrappers and furry slippers beside the fire, still others not dressed at all, nor seen, merely felt in the dark in the ultimate mystic intimacy, women not interfering with men's work but quietly standing, each beside her own man and seen by him only. Lookouts saw their faces in the stars or in the bending surface of the seas, firemen in their gauges. Men remembered special times and songs and places, mentally checked the payment of insurance premiums, wondered if the roof had been repaired where it leaked near the chimney and, if they didn't get back, if it would ever be repaired. A few thought, "Gee, Mom, I guess us kids batted you around a lot, but I sure love you..."

John Wohlschlaeger, with nothing to do but wait, began to write a letter. "Darling..." That was as far as he got. He was for the first time totally incommunicado. He was in a situation that words could not reach out of to someone who wasn't there with him. He sat there in lonely wonderment, staring at the sheet of paper that, but for the one word darling, remained blank.

Each department head was working out the alternative processes for his part of the ship under different conditions of damage. Captain Robinson, oddly enough, was for the moment placing himself in the position of the commander of the Japanese force. It was a quiet Sunday evening. Suddenly he was being fallen upon by an enemy striking force. What was he going to do? Order the whole scene illuminated and expose his vulnerable transports? Quickly. Quickly, he urged himself. Prompt decision. Very well, order half the destroyers and the light cruiser to engage the enemy close aboard, the rest of the convoy to ... do what? Get underway. To where? The attackers were probably accompanied by submarines. Get underway, nevertheless. Not sit there and be butchered like tethered pigs. But all this while time was passing. Torpedoes were plunging into his ships. And he dared not order all his escort vessels to close with the enemy since who was to say that, as soon as he did, an American reserve force would not rush among the then completely exposed transports and slaughter them?

Captain Robinson left this imaginary Japanese command with a feeling of satisfaction.

The striking force which he as OTC commanded would be up against overwhelming odds, but at least they were unencumbered, charged with the protection of nothing, while the Japanese commander would be embarrassed at every turn by the necessity to defend his fat transports and, so far at least as a large part of his warships was concerned, to abide with them.

The entrance to the anchorage where these ships lay would no doubt be mined. Lt. Commander Camp, the Chief Engineer, had seen to it that the water tanks in the ship's double bottom were full either of oil or water. That sheathing of noncompressible fluid was the ship's only armor from underwater blows, but it would help. Beyond that, there was nothing to do now besides hope.

In the wardroom an officer ordered coffee, watched to see if the cup trembled in the saucer, saw that it didn't, then, when the mess boy was gone, remarked to those beside him upon the quiet, nerveless stoicism of the Chinese. But when he lifted the cup to his lips, he found that it was empty.

The gunners were thinking of the *Marblehead* not in terms of its thousands of complex functions, but of the simple and direct one of throwing shells at the enemy. Each gun crewman was thinking of his own not small but definite task: the precision and speed with which his hands would seize upon and wrench the cans of 6-inch powder from the ready racks, the loaders who, in anticipation, felt each sent shell in their biceps, each of them full of an emotional certainty of hurling something destructive, something defiant but full of real, material protest against the enemy. The sent shell was hard and heavy in their straining arms. The impersonal destructiveness of each bag of powder was felt by every man who would handle it. But the most direct, not emotional but physical, sense of thrust at the enemy was existing in the imagination of the rammermen. They were the men who would strike the distant enemy with their fists, the men who would have the greatest physical sensation of standing there, slugging it out. These were the men who were really sending, and in the pits of their stomachs feeling sent, each shell. They were the ones who would die with the greatest sense of fulfilment if everything happened not to be entirely perfect.

In the sickbay, Chief Pharmacist's Mate Ace Evans now left the paregoric bottle out on the table. There had been a very light flare-up of dysentery in the late afternoon. Also, traffic at the drinking fountains was heavier than usual. Everybody, for some reason, was thirsty.

Aloft, in forward control, when Commander Van Bergen went to his station, he smiled very pleasantly to the enlisted men there: Chief Fire Controlman Raymond Edwards, Red Percifield, and two others. Van Bergen made that smile say, "If we keep on our toes, we'll make it somehow."

Van Bergen moved to a forward window, stood and looked out at the *Marblehead*'s slender, racing stem. His ultimate personal dream seemed very far away this evening. The bungalow on Pebble Beach. The little flat in San Francisco. Both presided over by a commuting male Chinese servant, an impeccable, properly clairvoyant Chinese such as Chang, Commander Goggins' superlative cabin boy. And then there was the sailboat, the 35-foot ketch, in which he and a friend, and this Chang-like Chinese servant, would start out in the Pacific to find ... what? ... Well, who could determine the form and texture of the

Golden Fleece, the panacea that would satisfy so many complicated hungers?

As he stood there in forward control on what might well be his last night, Van Bergen thought of something which had happened a night or two earlier, a little episode of the kind that may always overtake serious men of action, and one that had made him seem an ass. It was when he had dressed down a man for sitting down while on watch on the bridge.

"Just because it's dark here you needn't try to take advantage of the watch officers," Van Bergen had said sharply. "It's your duty to be on your toes both physically and mentally. I should think that if you had no respect for orders, you'd at least be intelligent enough to realize that when you cheat on your job you are unnecessarily endangering a ship on which you happen to be, shall we say, a passenger."

"But Mr. Van Bergen..."

"No excuses. You have been explicitly ordered to remain standing while on watch."

"I am standing, Mr. Van Bergen. You see, I... I just ain't very tall. I'm 'Shorty' Horning."

There had not been anything to say besides, "Sorry, Horning. Damn black night."

Well, tonight such little embarrassments were less than nothing. Both for Horning and for himself. Horning had, in all likelihood, never looked upon the gunnery officer as the personification of perfection anyway, and Van Bergen knew he'd been forgiven.

But nothing in the past had ever been like this tense, demanding, all-or-nothing present.

As the hours passed, men's minds in their focusing were themselves stripped for action. All of those parts of memory, the weighing of chances, all those aspects of their awareness not essential to their specific job ahead, had been, by the pressure of circumstance, cleared away. There was now only the utterly acute, the utterly crucial present. Then came news. The skipper's voice was heard over loudspeakers throughout the ship: "The enemy has moved. Due to the uncertainty of their position we are turning back. I'm sorry. Better luck next time."

No one really assimilated this news at the moment. Everybody was too tightly wound. Then they felt the ship take a slight list. She was turning back at twenty-one knots. Men looked at each other in strangely pained bewilderment.

On this, the *Marblehead*'s wedding night, the bride had disappeared.

AUSTRALIAN WAR MEMORIAL   OG3098

RAAF LIBERATORS BOMB BALIKPAN

PART 4

1

THE JAPANESE CONCENTRATION HAD MOVED, not retired nor been destroyed, and had still to be dealt with. On the afternoon of January 20th, while both the *Marblehead* and the *Boise* lay at anchor in Koepang Bay, a stir of excitement began to materialize inside the officers working on the coding boards. The Japanese force had been sighted heading toward Balikpapan. An attack was ordered. But it was to be led by the *Boise*. One of the *Marblehead*'s coding officers said, "Just our luck." The *Marblehead* had been having a little trouble with one of her turbines, but it was now repaired, and the ship was in fighting shape. Nevertheless, the *Boise* was given the job. Already destroyers were sliding out of their nests and coming over to fuel from the *Marblehead*. Why not? She wasn't going anywhere.

One of the first to arrive was the *Pillsbury*, which, the day before, had picked up a "contact" on her supersonics. The entire task force had hurriedly put to sea and the *Pillsbury* had staged a beautifully effective depth charge attack on a school of fish, which, as it turned out, had constituted her contact. The surface of the sea had soon become dotted with the most temptingly luscious tropical fishes. But since the *Pillsbury*'s skipper, "Froggy" Pound, had had no fuel for his motorboats, the *Bulmer* had stood in toward this windfall, lowered a boat, and hungrily gathered in the tropical fishes.

Today, once hoses were set, pumps started, and the refueling begun, the men on the *Marblehead* leaned over the lifelines looking down with envy and admiration at the combat-bound, devil-may-care seamen on the narrow little decks of the destroyers.

A man in dungarees and skivvy shirt, who was standing on the after deck house of the *Pillsbury*, yelled up at the men on the cruiser,

"Why don't you guys transfer off of that thing and join up with the fighting Navy?"

"We're scared to," Bull Aschenbrenner yelled. "We couldn't stand up to being shipmates with such tough guys as you."

This, from the Bull, fetched a roar of laughter from the rest of the *Marblehead* gang.

"Who with any brains," Ski Wardzinski shouted, "wants to bounce around in them God-damn tin cans?"

This was followed by a friendly crossfire of wholesome obscenity. Then somebody on the destroyer asked how the *Marblehead* was feeding these days.

"Sirloin steak every day," Barber Hawkins lied. "You guys must be pretty hard up to have to take the whole task force out to get a mess of fish."

Other of the *Marblehead*'s men asked when the *Pillsbury* was going to have another fish fry and how much they'd care to bid on a can of submarine turkey (salmon). Then Captain Pound started down the deck of the destroyer, and the men drifted back to their jobs.

By dusk the destroyers had been fueled, bringing the *Marblehead*'s oil supply down to forty percent, and all ships stood out of the harbor, the *Boise* group headed for their rendezvous with the enemy, the *Marblehead*, escorted by the *Bulmer*, going to Surabaya. As the ships left the harbor, Captain Robinson had the signal bridge wigwag, "Good luck."

That evening as the *Marblehead* steamed along to her unexciting destination, the Bull stood out on deck awhile and thought about home and particularly of his grandmother, who had raised him since his mother died when he was three months old. He called her Ma and she called him Shinny and had never believed he would reach the long pants stage without falling in the Minnesota River, a block away from their house, and drowning. But luck had been with her and she had managed to get him through the eighth grade of a Catholic school. After that he'd taken jobs on various farms around New Ulm, doing appalling amounts of work and making friends with everybody. Usually when he wasn't working, he was out fishing or hunting with his Uncle Joe.

Tonight, he just had to write home. He'd address the letter to his cousin Virginia, who would see that it got to all the family. He went to a table, laid his paper out on the scrubbed wood and wrote:

DEAR VIRGINIA:

THERE AIN'T MUCH TO WRITE AND YOU MUST EXCUSE THIS PAPER BUT THIS WAS ALL I COULD GET MY HANDS ON RIGHT NOW, BUT I ALWAYS SAY IT AIN'T THE PAPER THAT COUNTS IT'S THE WRITING THAT MAKES A PERSON FEEL GOOD AT HEART. WELL, HOW ARE YOU? I HOPE FINE AND I'M NOT SO BAD MYSELF. I STILL GOT HOPES I CAN DROP MY ANCHOR IN NEW ULM AGAIN SOMEDAY. VIRGINIA, I BET YOU FELT LIKE A BIG SHOT TO BE A BRIDESMAID. AND I BET JEANET WILL BE LIKE THE QUEEN OF SHEBA AFTER SHE GETS STUFFED INTO THAT OUTFIT YOU EXPLAINED TO ME. I SURE WAS GLAD TO GET THEM PAPER CLIPPINGS SO I COULD GET THE LOW DOWN ON THAT FIRE. I KNOW WHERE THAT FARM IS.

SAY HELLO TO MA AND I SURE AM GLAD TO HEAR SHE IS O.K. AGAIN. SAY DOES MA GET THOSE OUR NAVY MAGAZINES I AM SENDING? YOU CAN MAYBE GET ALL KINDS OF DOPE OUT OF THERE. I GET ONE EVERY MONTH BUT ALL I DO IS READ THE SCUTTLEBUTT SCANDAL AND THINGS LIKE A NEW COMMANDER IN CHIEF OF SOME FLEET BECAUSE THAT IS ONE THING WE ALWAYS HAVE TO KNOW. I THINK I SURE COULD GET AHEAD IN THE NAVY IF I

STAYED IN AND STUDIED HARD. BUT YOU KNOW IT'S JUST LIKE I USED TO BE IN SCHOOL, ALL FOOLISH TRICKS.

I SURE AM GETTING TO SEE SOMETHING OF THE WORLD SINCE I JOINED THE NAVY. YOU KNOW WHEN I WAS A FARMER ALL I SEEN WAS FIELDS AND ANIMALS AND MANURE PILES.

HANS, EVERY TIME I GET A PICTURE OF YOUR DAUGHTERS, I WISH I WASN'T RELATED TO THEM. I THINK I WILL HAVE TO DO SOME COURTING OR SOMETHING WHEN I GET HOME, IF I EVER GET HOME. IT SURE HURTS TO SEE ALL THOSE NICE YOUNG GIRLS IN NEW ULM GOING TO THE DOGS AND I HAVE TO BE DIGGING AROUND WITH EITHER A RUSSIAN OR CHINESE OR WHATEVER PORT WE ARE IN. AS A RULE, WE HAVE ONE IN EVERY PORT OR MAYBE TWO, HA HA. I ALWAYS SAID I HAVE A LIFE TO LIVE AND I SURE AM DOING IT.

SURE SORRY TO HEAR ABOUT WALLACE GETTING KILLED, HE MUST HAVE BEEN QUITE A MAN ALREADY. BUT YOU KNOW THE BRAVE DIE YOUNG. JUST WAIT TILL YOU READ ABOUT ME IN U. S. HISTORY. HA HA AGAIN.

BOY, I SURE WISH I COULD HAVE BEEN HOME TO BUTCHER AND HAVE SOME GOOD HOMEMADE SAUSAGE JUST LIKE MA USED TO MAKE IT. YOU KNOW ALL DAY I HAVE BEEN THINKING ABOUT SOME GOOD POTATO PANCAKES OR SOME HOMEMADE

SAUERKRAUT WITH PORK OR SMOKED SPARERIBS IN IT. M-M-M I CAN JUST SEE IT, BOY I'D GIVE A PAY DAY FOR JUST ONE MEAL. YOU DON'T KNOW HOW YOU CAN MISS SOMETHING LIKE THAT. WHERE SOME YEARS AGO I WAS TIRED OF. AND SUMMER, FISHING POLE ON MY BACK, STRAW HAT AND TRUCKING ALONG AND WHISTLING. THEM WERE THE DAYS BUT WE DIDN'T REALIZE IT.

I THINK A LOT OF ALL OF YOU. EVERY NIGHT BEFORE I FALL ASLEEP. AND TELL MA NOT TO WORRY. I AM O.K. AND ALWAYS WILL BE, I HOPE. I WOULD HAVE SENT YOU ALL A CHRISTMAS PRESENT BUT THE POSTAGE WAS SO MUCH I COULDN'T AFFORD IT BUT WHEN I COME BACK, I WILL BRING SOMETHING ALONG FOR ALL OF YOU. I SENT MA TEN BUCKS FOR A PRESENT; I THINK THAT WAS O.K. DON'T YOU?

THAT ROLLING STONE,

SHINNY.

LOVE AND KISSES XXXXXXXXXXXXXXXX TO ALL.

2

The *Boise* was due to pass through Sapi Strait at dawn. When she reached the Postilion Islands, she was to receive final instructions on the attack, but as she charged through Sapi Strait, there came a weird rumbling from below. The ship seemed to hesitate, shuddered, then passed clear. To the *Boise*'s First Lieutenant, Frederick J. Bell, it felt as if he were riding over a corduroy road in a Model-T Ford. Men who were below thought it was a near miss bomb explosion and started rushing up to man their battle stations. What had happened was that the *Boise* had struck a coral head. Her bottom was damaged, and it was plain she could not make the speed required for her mission.

Radio messages began to pass through the Pacific air. And excitement came back into being aboard the *Marblehead*. Her orders were to meet the *Boise* in Waworada Bay on the south side of Soembawa Island and fuel from her. Now apparently the cruiser force of the Asiatic Fleet consisted only of the *Houston* and the *Marblehead* until such time as the *Boise* could be repaired.

As the oil of the Boise was transfused into the *Marblehead*'s bunkers, Captain Robinson headed the board of inquiry which sat to fix the cause of this untimely casualty to the *Boise*'s bottom. Because, when a ship sent on a fighting mission is damaged en route to such an extent that the fight must be called off, her captain is in an extremely delicate and humiliating spot until a board of inquiry has met and established the blame. The board found that no blame could be placed on any of the *Boise* personnel, that it was simply a case of poorly charted waters.

In any case, the *Boise* was ordered to retire for repairs to the 116 feet of damaged bottom, and the *Marblehead* to cover a destroyer attack on the Japanese force in the Makassar Straits. Meanwhile, dapper Admiral Glassford moved his flag aboard the Ghost.

The attack was to occur on the night of January 24th. The *Marblehead* did not receive orders to sail until the 23rd; the distance to be covered was great; the weather in the Indian Ocean was bad. "We untied her," Red Percifield said, "and with one tin can leading, we headed for the clam bake. (The other destroyers, having a head start, were in a considerably advanced position.) Heavy weather held us down a bit in the Indian Ocean, but at last, late that afternoon we cut through the barrier into the mirror-like water of the Java Sea. Both ships got the bit in their teeth and laid back their ears. The can ran like a jackrabbit, but the 'Ghost' kept nipping at her heels. Those little four-pipers up ahead would need help aplenty once they started the fireworks."

The destroyers would start the fight all right, but the old *Marble-head* would finish it in case the destroyers had anything but the most terrific luck.

And up in forward control, eighty-eight feet above the water and topped only by the machine gun nest overhead, there was silence. Men knew the job ahead, how well it had to be done unless they were to be slaughtered, and there was nothing to say. Aside from orders, not twenty-five words were spoken in three hours.

Finally, somebody said, "In case we have to abandon ship, what'd we better do?"

"Just wait," Chief Fire Controlman Edwards said. "Wait and step out when the water comes up to meet us. Most of the explosions will be over by then, and the suction eased. If you try to jump from here, you might hit something."

"I guess that's best."

Hours passed. There was no message from nor contact with the destroyers somewhere ahead over the horizon. Captain Robinson ordered that a scouting plane be launched at dawn.

Long before daylight men began gassing and checking one of the little S.O.C. planes which sat upon the tracks of her catapult abaft the after stack and just forward of the mainmast. Small bombs nestled under each wing in case an enemy sub should be spotted. She was too slow and defenseless to fight anything else.

Half an hour before dawn Lt. E. M. Blessman was at the catapult checking over his instruments with a dimmed flashlight. Ten minutes later he kicked the motor over. It caught with a roar and sent long tongues of flame licking out of the exhausts.

Lt. Blessman was by no means a lad who'd learned to fly an airplane and then promptly regarded himself as one of the modern breed that would very soon make the battleship a thing of the past. There were some such young men at sea on Navy vessels at this period, and they frequently found themselves in a distinctly unsympathetic atmosphere in which seamen looked upon airmen as upstarts and in-terlopers, and airmen looked upon seamen as no doubt colorful but obsolescent hangovers from a time of technological darkness. But Lt. Blessman was not only an able and enthusiastic airman, he took his turn as officer of the deck at sea and stood a taut and dependable watch. It had never occurred to anybody in the wardroom to think of him as an outsider.

Now, as dawn grew near, Lt. Blessman spent fifteen minutes warm-ing his motor until the oil temperature was exactly where he wanted it, throttled her down, and yelled, "O.K., Tex." Tex Jennings, his radio man and gunner, who'd been climbing all over the fuselage making a last-minute inspection, pulled back the canopy and climbed in. While they slipped their parachute straps over their Mae Wests, the roar of the motor and the dull red of the exhaust pipe were heightened.

Both men got set squarely in their seats, backs and heads firmly against the seat behind them. Now just as the first flat gray light of dawn showed in the east, the throttle was opened. The plane quivered violently in its tugging against the catapult, then the 950-pound air charge in the catapult driving mechanism was released. The men's chests and stomachs flattened; the flesh of their jaws sagged back to-ward their necks as, within the space of a second or two, the plane was driven from zero miles per hour to sixty.

As the plane left the catapult, she dipped toward the water, recov-ered, and, at a shallow incline, began to climb into the gray-black sky.

Lt. Blessman felt that in all probability, Japanese land-based planes would be following such of the American destroyers as had survived the raid. If they were, he must get the news to the *Marblehead* at once. But if Japanese planes were coming, they would reach the *Marblehead* before the slow little S.O.C. could land and be recovered. Once the enemy planes started attacking the *Marblehead*, she'd begin the high-speed ducking and dodging called "radical evasion tactics." There would be no time to recover the scouting plane. If the attack outlasted his fuel supply, he'd have to hunt for some island beach and make a forced landing. If the enemy bombers were accompanied by fighters, the problem of gas supply would hardly matter. A Zero would kill the little S.O.C. as quickly and easily as a fox would kill a chicken.

As the plane clawed her way higher into the still-dim sky, both pilot and gunner focused their gaze on the unlit northward which held the answer to so many vital questions.

Tex Jennings thought he saw something. He picked up the intercom phone and said, "What's that off to the right of the nose?"

Blessman's gaze strained in that direction. His eyes picked up four wisps of white on the surface of the sea. "Ship wakes," he said.

A moment later a message was being received by the ship from Tex Jennings' blinker gun. It said, "All coming."

On the *Marblehead*, the immediate question was: all of what? The Japanese Navy? At this news, according to Percifield, "Powder cans were opened. A.A. ready boxes opened. Gun crews tightened their chin straps; lookouts tried to crawl through their glasses. Then over the horizon they came. The same four tin cans that had gone in to attack. But they weren't limping—they were driving headlong, bows high, sterns nearly awash, cocky. Still full of fight. A cheer went up from the *Marblehead*. As we swung in behind them, placing our A.A. guns between them and the north, they made their report. Tojo had been caught with his bloomers adrift and these four bantams had thrown everything in his lap but the garbage. They had gotten in so close they shot his searchlights out with .50 calibre machine guns. Some of the torpedoes had been fired at such close range that, when they exploded against the sides of the Japanese ships, the concussion knocked the destroyer officers down on the deck. What a riot. Uncle had served out a new kind of fish that night and the supermen didn't like them.

"Keep a sharp look out." Orders from the bridge. Look out for what? Again gun-crews touched their chin straps. Nerves tingled; eyes strained.

"Suddenly a crashing roar! Gun crews fell flat. They had seen nothing. Yet. The safety valve on No. 1 boiler had lifted and all the fury of hell broke loose, roared from the exhaust. The men looked at each other. They started to grin. Then they roared. 'Too-hoo, Gertrude!

Were you frightened?' one called. Another retorted, 'You didn't look like Gen. Jackson yourself trying to dig a hole in that steel deck.'

"That did it. Everything was O.K. Bring 'em on. We're ready. But the only thing we saw was a B-17. He came from the north and flashed a signal as he passed."

By breakfast time, the *Marblehead* was slowing to twelve knots. Lt. Blessman and Tex Jennings were gliding down onto the landing strip of smooth water created by the ship's wake. Then once the plane touched water, it taxied up that wake, was hoisted aboard, and a few minutes later its two men crawled out and were on their way to eat scrambled eggs and toast and coffee.

What, precisely, had the attack accomplished?

According to the destroyer division commander's message, seven enemy ships had been sunk, and an undetermined number damaged.

3

While the attack of the 24th made a worthwhile dent in the Japanese force, it was nevertheless but a single round in a running fight. That round had gone to the American Navy, but the advance of the Japanese had not been stopped. A heavier blow had to be struck.

On January 31st, the *Marblehead* again was ordered to stand by for an attack on Balikpapan. The enemy force there consisted of two cruisers, twelve destroyers and a number of transports. Admiral Glassford, meanwhile, had removed his flag from the *Marblehead*, which had been a flagship for little more than a day. The attack was scheduled to occur at 3:30 Sunday morning. By now Sunday had begun to be the *Marblehead*'s day of destiny. All her attacks and planned attacks had been on Sunday.

The plan of attack, developed while the ship was underway for the target area, was for the destroyers to lead the attack, traveling fast in in-line formation using "curved fire ahead" with torpedoes. The *Marblehead* was to support with her main battery. Then, as the destroyers retired, the cruiser was to get on the tail of the line, let go with her own torpedoes, and cover the retirement.

Throughout the afternoon the striking force was clocking off 100 sea miles every four hours. Late in the afternoon, one of the lookouts thought he saw an airplane in the distance off the starboard hand. But when questioned, he said he couldn't be sure.

He had. This Japanese plane saw the striking force and relayed the news to the Japanese commander in Balikpapan. The reception was being swiftly and forcefully prepared. Five more cruisers and a number of submarines were ordered to Balikpapan immediately. By sundown this powerful force was deployed to catch the little American striking force in a crossfire that should accomplish its destruction in something less than five minutes. And the *Marblehead* and her destroyers were steaming toward this trap at twenty-five knots. She could not send scouting planes ahead because if catapult planes were sighted by the enemy, they could only mean that an American task force was somewhere within the limited range of these planes.

As the ship plowed along, Tex Owens and W. A. Patterson, both electrician's mates and both Texans, were back in the ram room arguing about Mexican food. The ram room housed the big hydraulic rams which drove the rudder yoke which in turn controlled the rudder, upon which the ship's maneuverability depended.

"You talk about elegant vittles," Patterson said, "they don't come any better than the stuffed peppers at the Carta Blanca in San Antonio. Down on Houston Street near the hospital. They got a little nervous-nelly waiter in there that I bet's toted more good chow than any man alive."

"Maybe so," Tex Owens said dreamily. "Me, I'd settle right now for about a quart of good chili like they've usually got warming on the back of the stove in a cafe in my hometown."

He could see that cafe as he talked: the scanty rack of magazines, the pinball machine and juke box. A man at the counter drinking beer, wearing high-heeled boots, whose brown sweaty shirttail had worked up almost past his belt. Now the bus was stopping outside, and a lot of tired-looking people were coming in the cafe, standing and stretching their legs while they waited for sandwiches. Tex pointedly avoided thinking how far away all that was.

At one of the starboard A. A. guns the crew was singing The Sidewalks of New York. Then when the song was finished, men from different states requested Georgia on My Mind, Wabash Moon, Beautiful Ohio, Alabamy Bound.

In the crew's quarters one man was shining his shoes in anticipation of forthcoming inspections. Where one group was talking, Raymond E. Edwards was explaining the meaning of his middle initial. He was the youngest child in a large family, and his parents, wishing to go on record and to make things clear, had given him the middle name: Enough. Lt. Commander Morris Smellow, the supply officer, was checking his storeroom supplies and learning with dismay that the remaining supply of fresh eggs would hardly last more than a week.

A week? When the ship was going into battle this very night?

After all, this was the crew's third sortie. Twice before, something had caused them to survive. No longer was this time of impending battle quite so much a part of the unknown. What had been done twice could be done again. Though these men had not yet fired a shot at the enemy, the war was two months' less new and disquieting than it had been in the beginning. Tonight, they'd shoot up Balikpapan and make a getaway of some kind.

At his battle station with the forward repair party, Bull Aschenbrenner was realizing that tomorrow was Sunday and that again there would be no "Happy Hour," as there always had been every Sunday evening until the last two before war started.

Happy Hour was the bluejackets' prerogative, a little period of entertainment every Sunday evening immediately following the usual Sunday night repast of cold cuts. Red Percifield, whom the Bull thought was killingly funny, usually acted as master of ceremonies. Red wrote most of the songs and jokes and skits which were, almost without fail, satisfyingly dirty. Radio Striker P. P. Hill was Red's star comedian and could make his shipmates howl. He also performed entertainingly on the washboard, the one percussion instrument in Tex Owens' band, which consisted of five guitars, two fiddles, and a varying number of French harps.

The songs P. P. Hill sang were usually parodies on such old numbers as The Monkeys Have No Tails in Zambo Ango, revamped to contain such gossipy quatrains as:

> The girls wear no teddies in Manila,
>
> The girls they wear no teddies in Manila,
>
> The girls they wear no teddies,
>
> they're a bunch of ever-readies,
>
> Oh, the girls they wear no teddies in Manila.

Too, there were a lot of jokes about bald-headed men and pregnant women, and others which put the finger on the eccentricities of certain of the officers and prominent members of the crew.

There was also community singing at which time the Bull enjoyed braying lustily. But now with this infernal war on, Happy Hour was just a pleasant memory.

The captain was dining alone, as usual, from a tray in his little sea cabin, bare as a monk's cell though hardly as large. He was not hungry and only ate a few bites and drank a cup of coffee.

But in that time, as he had so often done before, he realized how completely alone he was. Everybody had somebody else to go to when things began to come apart. He had only himself. From now until the fight was over, he alone was entirely responsible for every man's life, every man's actions, the efficacy of his little task force within the framework of the war. Imagine any one man being truly able to meet the demands of so much responsibility. He meant to smile, but the muscles in his face didn't move. This job made no allowances for human frailty. True, he had good officers. But, ultimately, in accepting his command, he'd signed an unwritten guarantee that he'd make the most of any opportunity, avoid each of the thousands of errors into which he might fall.

He thought of Admiral Hart and the really outstanding intelligence with which he had handled his little Asiatic Fleet prior to the opening of hostilities. On Sunday, November 25th, Admiral Hart had called a special conference of his skippers and said he felt an attack was imminent and wanted his forces deployed.

Captain Robinson could not help remembering the force and decision in that small, careful, incredibly determined man. He said very little, but his mind worked in terms of hard reality. Captain Robinson knew he was a man who could be counted on to the last.

Even as far back as April 1941, Admiral Hart had got his people out of the habit of being in port in Manila Bay over the weekend. Sunday, throughout military history during the Christian period, had been the principal day for surprise attack. Moreover, whenever during the week there was a small crisis of any kind, Admiral Hart scattered his fleet. Well, Admiral Hart had done his job, and was still doing it. Now, with the most flexible orders, it was up to Captain Robinson, and the thousand-plus Yankees at his command, to play the part of David, and play it well or die.

But in any case, the thing was not to tighten up.

He found himself remembering a few lines Admiral Hart had passed on to him months earlier, a prayer on which Hart had leaned whenever he was up against anything that seemed too big to handle. "Dear God," Captain Robinson repeated now, "give us the strength to accept with serenity the things that cannot be changed. Give us the courage to change the things that can and should be changed. And give us the wisdom to distinguish the one from the other."

He took his last swallow of coffee, unconsciously put his cap on at a rakish angle, and went out on the bridge, humming a sprightly tune.

The night out there was bright and noncommittal. The captain thought how easily a Japanese reconnaissance plane might sight the striking force.

Commander Goggins was on the bridge.

"Bill," the captain said, "there are many times when an old sailor has much less use for moonlight than a younger one."

Commander Goggins grunted.

But despite the fact that the Japanese controlled the air, there was a lone long-range Navy scouting bomber in the air. It dared not come in too close range of the Japanese fighter planes at Balikpapan, but just at dusk it peeped over the horizon, saw the trap that had been set, and reported it to American headquarters in Surabaya which, in turn, got the word to the striking force.

Realizing that to persist in the attack meant throwing away both his men and his ships without adequate return, Captain Robinson ordered a reversal of course. He was going back to get more guns.

As the turn was begun, one of the officers was taking a look around to see that no lights were showing. In passing one of the 3-inch guns he heard one man angrily demand, "Who gave that order for us to turn back?"

A man beside him said, "The skipper."

"Well, that's O.K.," the first voice said. "But we don't want none of those shore-based sons of bitches telling us what to do."

The officer smiled and went on, unrecognized, to finish his inspection.

AERIAL VIEW OF INTRAMUROS, MANILA, MAY 1945.

4

The following day, Sunday, in a spectacularly violent rainstorm, the *Marblehead* rendezvoused with the heavy cruiser *Houston*, Captain Rooks commanding. Nine 8-inch guns had been added to the striking force. There were more to come.

This was February 1st. Captain Robinson wrote: "Cruising off Madura Strait awaiting developments. I now have the *Houston* and six destroyers under my command. What next?"

The following day he added: "Still standing by. I feel it's the lull before the storm. The battle of Makassar Straits will culminate soon."

At eight o'clock that day, orders arrived for the American ships to proceed to Madura Straits and rendezvous with the Dutch flagship *De Ruyter*, carrying Admiral Doorman.

However, on the afternoon of February 3rd, a flight of about forty Japanese bombers passed over at great altitude on its way to bomb Surabaya. Only one plane lingered behind to get accurate reconnaissance data on the ships.

At midnight the *Marblehead* which, earlier in the evening, had received aboard a local Reserve Officer, Sub-Lieutenant Luxemburg, for liaison, stood out to sea in company with the *Houston*, the *De Ruyter*, the *Tromp* and seven Dutch and American destroyers, under Admiral Doorman's command.

Both of the Dutch cruisers were smaller than the *Marblehead*. The *De Ruyter* was a 6,400-ton vessel, and the *Tromp*, at a little over 3,000 tons and carrying six 5.9-inch guns, was actually less a cruiser than a kind of super-destroyer. But both ships were new and fast and highly welcome force-mates for the American ships. As a matter of fact, Japan had some fifteen cruisers among her older ships, some of which might compose the force at Balikpapan, that either the *Tromp* or *De Ruyter* could fight ship-for-ship and on even terms.

At the other side of the picture, the Japanese had eight heavy cruisers which, with ten 8-inch guns, outgunned the *Houston* or any other cruiser in the American fleet except the Pensacola and the Salt Lake City. But since the whole American position had been reduced to a hit-run program of raiding, with the purpose of delaying and holding the Japanese, the force now collected off Bali was a formidable and a serious menace to the enemy at Balikpapan. Had the American force been in possession of enough aircraft so that, as the surface ships closed with the enemy vessels, command of the air might have been at least in dispute, this Dutch and American force would have been in a position to attack the force at Balikpapan on fairly equal terms. But aside from its few virtually unarmed scouting and patrol craft, it was completely without any means of engaging the enemy in the air.

Dawn broke red, burnishing the bottoms of clouds that floated across the sky before a mild westerly breeze. Occasionally through the broken clouds the sky lookouts could see the high mountains of Bali looming in the distance. Men washed up and breakfasted as usual, were mustered on stations at eight o'clock. They turned to and went to work on routine ship's business immediately afterward. Sky control and a part of the antiaircraft battery had been in a constant condition of readiness ever since war began.

Then a little after nine o'clock a messenger on the *De Ruyter* ran to Admiral Doorman with a dispatch from Surabaya.

At once he ordered the following message flashed to all ships: "37 bombers to Surabaya, course SSW. Report timed 0810."

But by the time this message could reach Captain Robinson the *Houston* was signaling, "Strange aircraft sighted bearing 023 true." At the same time a lookout on the *Marblehead* yelled, "Planes approaching from the east." Those with glasses could see them approaching at about 17,000 feet, that the planes were twin-engined, twin-tail heavy monoplane bombers. By now it was possible to detect the unusually high dihedral of the wings which had the shape of the German JU-86K. But the noses were less prominent than that of the German plane. On the wings and tail of each was the red sun of Japan.

Already the surface ships were beginning, according to doctrine, to scatter. On the bridge of the *Marblehead*, Captain Robinson was snapping out orders that were being relayed by talkers through their telephone chest sets and thence throughout the ship. The general alarm was set off. Over the loudspeaker were coming the words: "Air defense—man your battle stations."

When Warrant Electrician Jarvis heard the bugler sound air defense, he himself was topside standing near the port torpedo tubes. But he'd heard air defense sounded so often that it caused no tingle in his spine. He looked up to the signal yard to see what the hoist was. There was nothing there. But he did see the air defense crew peering into the sky, and his gaze followed the direction in which their binoculars pointed. His heart started to pound. He saw a great number of specks that were unmistakably planes. Instantly he knew there were too many of them to be ours. He started running to his room for his flashlight and his wallet.

In every passageway and compartment men were going into action. Cooks were cutting out galley fires, mess men tearing off their aprons as they ran to ladders and started down. Each time they passed below a deck a steel hatch clanged shut above them. Seamen overhead spun the locking wheels which caused steel dogs to extend from the hatch covers and make the hatch cover one with the decks. As magazine crews reached the bottom of the ship, powder magazines were unlocked. Ammunition trains for the A.A. guns began to move. Men in the fire rooms lighted off the remaining six boilers. The order had come for maximum power in the shortest possible time. There was already enough steam for twenty-seven knots. Valves turned and the streams of black oil flowed faster into the roaring fireboxes. Doctors and hospital corpsmen were evacuating the sick from the more exposed sickbay to a better protected part of the ship. Officers strapped on their pistols. Damage control parties ran to their stations to wait, locked in, to fight out the sea when it should start into the ship. Men poured into the 6-inch mounts, dragged shut the steel doors and dogged them down. Everywhere doors clanged, were locked as the ship was made tight. Over the loudspeakers was coming the recurrent order, "Set condition Zed," which meant, close ship, lock all watertight compartments.

Topside the yard-long shells flowed from man to man to the 3-inch guns. Gunners strapped down their helmets over their chins so that the blast of the guns would not carry the helmets away. Codebooks were ready to be dropped over the side in weighted bags. Back aft, Machinist's Mate Dale Johnson was jettisoning 4,000 gallons of aviation gas into the sea.

17,000 feet up, the first wave of nine Japanese planes had started their power glide on the ship.

As the preaching hot-shellman reached his station, he looked in the sky, pointed to his long, heavy asbestos gauntlets and said, "Hand me those gloves. Here is some killing the Lord will forgive."

5

As Captain Robinson brought his ship right, in accordance with the scatter plan, Commander Van Bergen was watching the enemy.

"They're dividing into squadrons, Captain. Apparently one for each cruiser. One squadron is heading this way."

"Very well." Then to the quartermaster: "Steady her on 85 true."

"Aye, aye, sir. Steady her on 85 true."

"Captain," it was Commander Van Bergen, "I think they are about to start their run on us."

The captain turned to the seaman at the engine room telegraph. "All engines ahead full."

"All engines ahead full, sir."

The Captain beckoned to young Bishop, the ship's junior aviator, who had come to the bridge for a better view of the scrap.

"Bishop, keep your eyes peeled on those planes and give me the word about a minute and a half before bomb release so I can maneuver out of trouble."

Bishop grabbed his glasses and glued his eyes to the sky.

"They're at their release point, Captain."

"Give her left full rudder, Quartermaster."

"Left full rudder, sir," as the wheel spun.

Very carefully the quartermaster of the watch was writing down each alteration of course and speed in the log. Down in the ram room where Tex Owens was on watch in place of his friend Patterson who was on the sick list, he saw the starboard ram drive the arm of the rudder yoke a full stroke backward and felt the ship heel to starboard as she began her fast port turn.

Topside the 3-inch A.A.'s began kicking the deck and sending their projectiles tearing through the air. Each gun at the moment of firing looked like a geranium blossoming on a long gray stem. As the range decreased, the fuse setters reduced the time at which the shells would explode after leaving the gun, so that overhead it appeared that the planes were climbing down a stairway of brown-black puffs. Now there were two waves making their runs on the *Marblehead*, nine in the first wave, eight in the second.

Then both waves passed over the *Marblehead* at 14,000 feet without dropping bombs.

A few seconds later, the planes were out of range and the 3-inch guns ceased firing.

"They must be testing the ceiling of our flak," Captain Robinson remarked.

"Captain," Commander Van Bergen said, "there are eight more planes approaching on the port bow."

Thirty-five seconds later the talkers at each gun were relaying the order, "Open fire."

As the shooting was resumed, the engines were pushed up to flank speed. And again, the great rams drove the rudder hard left. A hundred and seventy-five seconds later the Japs had passed over and were out of range, still having dropped no bombs.

Meanwhile, in forward repair, Bull Aschenbrenner begged so hard to be allowed to watch a minute or two of the shooting that he got special permission to go topside. As he came out on deck, the *Marblehead* was splitting through the water at twenty-nine knots. He saw nine planes start their run, saw the A.A. shells going up to meet them.

On the bridge, Bishop said, "Captain, they're at their release point."

"Right rudder fifteen degrees. Tell engine room all speed possible."

The order was repeated and executed.

Now, in a very quiet voice, Van Bergen said, "The bombs have been released, sir. It's going to be close."

Over the loudspeaker came: "Seek cover. Bombs coming. Lie flat."

All hands not required by their jobs to remain topside had been ordered below, since the Japanese had in recent engagements been using anti-personnel bombs that exploded on contact with the first solid object they encountered.

When Van Bergen had said this stick of bombs was going to be close, he was right. The sound of plunging bombs cutting through the air whispered in his ear. The sea rose and erupted. Men atop the foremast were drenched. The bombs had smashed into the water and exploded sixty-five yards away.

But as the planes passed over, one of them began to smoke and the A.A. gunners to whoop and yell.

Then the pilot in the crippled plane, unable to hold altitude, decided he'd make his wounded plane and the rest of his bombs count. He put her nose down, banked and started diving, smoking, into the *Marblehead*, as all her guns gave him their maximum volume of fire. Word went below to the repair parties to move to the starboard side, since torpedoes were expected from port. Then as the plane drove on in toward the ship and passed within range of the .50 calibre machine guns, the gunners began stitching their tracers into the cockpit of the plane. In its rushing, roaring, increasing nearness it seemed the size of a house. But the stream of lead going into it was heavy and incessant and merciless. Suddenly it turned straight down and crashed into the water. The *Marblehead* crew broke into wild cheering.

The Bull tore back to his station and yelled, "We just got a great big bastard!"

Yeoman Beauford Gabriel had seen the planes coming as he ran to his station on the main deck forward of the wardroom where he passed 3-inch ammunition aft to the A.A. guns. When the firing began overhead, he felt queasy in the stomach, but soon the ammunition was coming so fast that there was hardly the time to be concerned with his own feelings. He made several trips to the guns with boxes of ammunition before he was shifted to the line that was hauling the boxes up from below to the main deck.

At first, he heard only the 3-inch battery firing. Then the machine guns cut loose, and all the men below decks knew that planes had come in at very close range.

In the improvised sickbay in the torpedo workshop, the pipe-rimmed wall bunks were being readied to receive the wounded.

Instruments, in pockets on a wide stretch of canvas, were hung against the bulkheads. Morphine and tannic acid were at hand.

As Dr. Ryan worked beside Pharmacist's Mate Ace Evans he said, "It's too bad this attack caught many of the men half-dressed. If we get hit, that's going to make the burns worse."

Since ship's business and condition watches go on day and night, it was naturally necessary for those with night watches to sleep during the day. Many of the men who'd been awakened by the general alarm were fighting in their skivvies.

By now Commander Goggins, who'd been aft to make sure the aviation gasoline had been jettisoned, had finished his inspection of the decks and had reached the wardroom. Lt. Blessman, the flier, and two or three others were congregated there when Mr. Smellow, the supply officer, came in and said, "Why don't you fellows scatter out? We might take a hit here and we're going to need as many live officers as we can muster."

Mr. Smellow, having no air defense duties, went on to his room, lit his pipe, and sat down to sweat out the fight.

Other men down in the magazines, Chinese and Americans, surrounded by enough gunpowder to break the ship into pellets, also, except for those men handling 3-inch ammunition, had nothing to do but wait.

Earlier that morning, at 9:55, when the fight had been only six minutes old, Hing, the captain's boy, had abandoned his post in the ammunition train.

"Hey, you!" a petty officer had yelled. "Get the hell back in line and keep on passing them shells."

"Very sorry," Hing had said, hurrying away. "Captain have coffee every morning at ten o'clock."

With that he was gone. Five minutes later he'd served coffee to Captain Robinson who, hardly noticing what he was doing, had drunk it. Then when Hing had returned the cup and tray to the pantry, he had gone below and again taken up his work in the ammunition train.

After Warrant Electrician Jarvis had got his wallet and flashlight, he had started toward the electrical shop and met the engineering officer coming sleepily from his room.

"What's all the racket about?" Mr. Camp had asked. "Another false alarm?"

"The sky is full of Jap planes."

Mr. Camp's half-open eyes grew huge with realization and he started running to his station in the forward engine room.

When Walter Jarvis reached the electrical shop, he found most of his electricians gathered there, and at once realized the danger of such a concentration. A direct hit would kill them all and the ship would be without electricians. He told them to scatter, then saw three men who should have been in the Interior Communications Room in the bottom of the ship. They said they'd been locked out. He told these men to wait where they were and went to see if it were possible to get them below without opening too many watertight doors. He found it was too late to get them there, started back to the electrical shop, and just as he reached it, heard the loudspeaker blaring, "Bombs coming. Lie flat." He made it to a bench inside the shop and spread out flat on top of it.

The time now was exactly 10:25. A wave of eight planes was beginning their bombing run. The ship's position was latitude 7° 23' 30' south, longitude 115° 46' 30' east.

On the bridge, as the guns once more started firing, Commander Van Bergen said, "Release point reached..."

At 10:26 Quartermaster of the Watch Grant, who sat on the deck tailor-fashion with his log, wrote, "Eight planes passed overhead."

As he wrote, the bombs had already started their curving trajectory, aimed straight for the *Marblehead*'s naked decks.

Captain Robinson and all the other men topside watched the bombs coming and could see they were not going to miss.

Over the loudspeakers came, "Seek cover. Lie flat."

Ski Wardzinski, who had so long been convinced that his own death was imminent, had sunk to his knees between the catapults a moment earlier and said, "God, please don't let them hit us." He had just regained his feet and gone back to work when the bombs struck home and the *Marblehead* leaped, racked and twisting, into the air.

The men on the *Houston*'s bridge thought they saw daylight between the *Marblehead*'s keel and the sea. Then the ship was engulfed in a blinding flash, and she disappeared behind a wall of fire and water.

The *Houston*'s quartermaster shook his head and said, "There goes the *Marblehead*."

MANILA CITIZENS FLEE FROM SUBURBS BURNED BY JAPANESE
SOLDIERS, 10 FEBRUARY 1945.

PART 5

1

AT THE MOMENT OF IMPACT, the *Marblehead* leaped out of the sea like a wild horse. By clinging desperately to the wheel, Helmsman Kelly, alone among those on the bridge, managed not to be thrown on the deck. By the time Captain Robinson got to his feet he saw that his ship was afire aft and amidships, that she was burning furiously and that heavy columns of black smoke, such as emanate from oil or paint fires, were pouring out of her. He could also sense a peculiar and sickening kind of deadness and shocking loss of vitality that was coming over the ship. His whole consciousness was being bludgeoned with the realization of it. He knew what was causing it. She was, with terrifying swiftness, losing buoyancy. The sea was pouring into her and flooding her.

"Find out how bad the engines have been hurt," Captain Robinson called to his engine room talker. The engine rooms were her heart.

"Out of communication with the engine room, sir." All other talkers were likewise out of communication.

"Captain!" It was Quartermaster Kelly. "We've lost steering control, sir. Rudder jammed hard left."

The ship was circling madly to the left. Yet as men pulled themselves upright, the guns began to fire again.

The captain turned to Van Bergen. "Find out what's happened, Nick. How badly hurt we are. What can be done."

"Aye, aye, sir."

Van Bergen left the bridge at a run.

If only there had been some communications lines open so he'd know where to go first. There must be some sort of trouble in the Interior Communications room among others.

There was.

The only man who'd been in the Interior Communications room was an electrician named Sevey. The I.C. room was on the port side near the bottom of the ship.

It had been located there because, electrically speaking, it was the ship's spinal cord and because, in an engagement either with surface ships or with planes, this presumably would be one of the best protected spots on the ship. Not only did this room contain the motor generators, but the three vital switchboards: the power transfer board, the navigation board, and the interior communications board, each of these covering a whole side of the room.

Sevey had been working at the interior communications board when the ship was hit. The big switchboard left the bulkhead, struck him, and knocked him eighteen feet where he fetched up violently against the after bulkhead. The lights had gone out. Sevey was entangled in the wire of his battle phones. Water was rushing into the ink-black room and covering him.

As fast as he could move, he climbed to the overhead hatch, began undogging it, and climbed out. But the water was rising so fast that, as he tried to close the hatch, the rising flood driving out the air which had previously occupied the room would not permit the hatch to close. Suddenly the horrifying realization came upon Sevey that his own small strength was now directly matched against the plangent power of the sea. Unless the hatch could be closed and dogged down, the water would continue to run into the ship and perhaps sink her.

Sevey had no way to know whether the watertight doors had been blown away from the surrounding compartments. Saving the ship might very well depend on his own actions at this moment.

Yet no matter how hard he pressed, the upward-rushing air held open the hatch. Finally realizing that his own strength was insufficient, he stopped pressing, raised the hatch, took a firm grip on the locking wheel, gathered all his strength, put his body close against the hatch, ready to spin the wheel the instant the slamming hatch might touch the deck, and threw his body and the hatch downward. Their combined weight, force and momentum drove the hatch momentarily to the deck, and before it could bounce back from this rubbery cushion of compressing air the wheel spun, the dogs reached out and caught. Sevey hurried off to report that the I.C. room was wrecked and flooded.

2

In Central Station, which was adjacent to the I.C. room, and which was the headquarters and central directing point for coordinating damage control, the officer in charge was twenty-six-year-old Frank Blasdel. There was also a repair party of several enlisted men present.

Suddenly there was a terrific crash and shock. Frank Blasdel was in the air. The first thing that came to his mind was that the Central Station, seen from some distance up in the air, looked peculiarly unlike itself. And while still in the air there came to his mind the memory of a battle report about a man who'd been sitting on the toilet when his ship struck a mine. Upward shock had thrown the man against the overhead. This blow had stunned him. But the same force which had thrown him upward had, at the same time, shattered the porcelain toilet bowl so that when the man fell back down, he landed among the jagged porcelain spears and was castrated. Frank Blasdel at this moment, with this terrible picture in his mind, was looking for a place to land. Then he crashed down on the deck.

The question in the faces of all the men who were now strewn about the Station was: what's happened?

"We've probably been hit by a torpedo," Frank Blasdel said, drawing the logical inference from the generally upward thrust of the blow.

He ordered the men to stand back from the gyrocompass, which had been thrown out of its gimbals. Inside that compass was a twenty-pound balance wheel turning at 9,000 revolutions a minute. If its bearings were damaged, it might at any second now tear itself free and go wild in the room.

When Frank Blasdel tried to get in touch with his boss, Lt. Commander Drury, he found that the phones were out, and, a few minutes later, when water began running out of the voice tube which led to the I.C. room, he knew why. Too, by the heat he knew that fires were raging overhead and that he'd better get his people out as fast as he could.

Meanwhile one of his men slammed shut a magazine scuttle which was open and spun the locking wheel.

"Wait," another man said. "I think I hear someone down there."

They spun it open and out came five men of the magazine crew.

Blasdel decided to try to find some means of egress through the fire. If he could get through it, he would (1) find a way to get his men out, and (2) get permission from Mr. Drury to abandon station. He began to wet down his clothes, a sweatshirt and a pair of dungarees in which he'd been doing calisthenics when the engagement began and started up through the fire. By this time water was already knee-deep in the Central Station.

On the deck above, he crawled as far as he could through the smoke but found at the end of every path fire through which no man could pass and live. Frank turned back, went into the Central Station, and dogged down the hatch behind him.

The report he gave to his men was simply, "No soap."

He looked up at the cable-and-voice-tube-cluttered hollow leg of the tripod mainmast, the lower end of which began in the overhead of this Station. It was a 40-foot climb up to the first outlet. It had originally been designed as an escape tube but had subsequently come to contain many cables and voice tubes. Perhaps a small man could wriggle through it. And then he turned and looked at Joe DeLude, the tailor. Joe was bigger than the hole. A decision had to be reached at once.

"We'll abandon station," Frank Blasdel said, looking just to the left of Joe DeLude, "by means of the tripod leg. It'll be a tight fit. We'll leave in order of size. The smallest man first. You there, start up. Somebody give him a boost."

The smallest man hunched his shoulders, was jammed up the narrow opening, caught hold of the rungs inside and, like a large ant in a cluttered drinking straw, started squirming his way up.

A tall, skinny man was next. And while his body would fit into the tube, his legs were so long that he could not bend his knees sufficiently to raise his feet to the succeeding rung. Frank Blasdel, who went in just under him, caught his feet and thrust them, knowing the man's knees were being battered to pieces, up to the next rung.

And finally, they were all gone except Joe DeLude, who was waist-deep in the rising water. He piled up furniture under the opening in the overhead. By exhaling and holding both arms straight above his head and jammed hard against his ears, he was finally able to work his shoulders into the mast leg.

When Joe grabbed the next rung and dragged himself a few inches upward, his feet were dangling, and the bottom of the mast leg closed around the upper part of his hips and held him.

Joe was all alone now. Nobody could help him. The ship was afire and sinking. He was out of touch with all his fellows. This 40-foot tube was the only path that led to survival. And it was too small. He was desperate. Inside his body, the adrenal glands were secreting that fluid which gives all animals a last spurt of illogically great strength. And he clawed with such violence that his fat buttocks were finally mashed inside the tripod leg. By the most superhuman effort he was able to drag himself six or seven feet before the junction of a great number of cables closed in upon him and wedged him fast.

JUNKERS JU-86

3

As the ship was hit, machinist's mate Dale Johnson was at the midships repair station, on the starboard side of the main deck. The first sound he heard after the explosion was someone screaming, "I'm dying!" over and over again. By this time, he was on his feet and several men were rushing to the sound of the screams. But he got in front of them and told them to start fighting the fire with extinguishers and hoses and to help the wounded later.

One man who'd been lying on the deck near Johnson had been blown fifty feet to the end of the passageway. Another man, forward of Johnson, had been leaning over drinking from a water-fountain. The fountain, about the size of an ordinary gas range, had been blown out from under his drinking mouth across an areaway and through the wall of the post office. When the man stood up, his arm was singed, and his right ear burned off by the sharply stratified flash.

Chief Bos'n Harvey Andersen was almost out of action. When the ship was hit, the shock had thrown a 6-inch shell out of its rack and sent it crashing against his ankle.

Ski Wardzinski, to his own great amazement, was still alive and unhurt. He ran below to find a job to do.

Yeoman Beauford Gabriel was looking through the ship to see whether his brother Ralph was dead or alive. At this time, he was coming into the forward citadel, the area between the two upper 6-inch guns, where many of the wounded were laid out, and was looking from face to face to see whether Ralph was among them. Then he heard someone call his name and looked around. It was Ralph, and he was uninjured. But hardly had Beauford been swept by the great surge of relief he felt on seeing Ralph, when Ralph knelt down beside one of the injured men. As Beauford got over to them, he found it was their old friend Dave Hodges.

A corpsman was pumping morphine into Dave's charred body.

"Gee," Ralph said, doing his best to control his voice, "it's too bad you got singed like that, Dave. You better lie there and take it easy for an hour or two. We got some things to do, but we'll drop back after a while. Just take it easy, kid. You'll be O.K."

And both of the Gabriel boys went off to fight the fires, knowing their friend was dying.

Up in forward control, atop the foremast, the terrific lurch had created a whip effect in the mast, like that in the shaft of a golf club as it strikes the ball. There had been a number of boxes of .50 calibre ammunition, which the men used as seats and which would, when necessary, be passed up to the machine gunners who were firing from the foretop. The whip in the mast had thrown these boxes and people violently about, and all the men in the station were injured and bleeding. But seeing they were no longer needed, since the main battery would not be employed and since there was no communication and their director was wrecked, they started down the mast to lend a hand where they could.

The midships blast had caught Commander Goggins in the wardroom where he was watching the ammunition party to see that they kept in order. Blood ran from an egg-sized hole in the back of his neck and flash burns had seared his flesh wherever it was exposed. Picking himself up, he started on the first lap of an inspection that was to cover the whole ship before he reported the extent of the damage to the bridge.

As he walked, his skin began turning from a pale tan to a bright lobster red and then began to drop off in patches. Smoke and steam and flame reached out from the No. 1 hatch, but he managed to crawl aft. Wherever he turned, debris was piled high, blocking his way. He reached Battle Two but could raise no one there, then climbed down again to No. 3 hatch to see if anything could be done about the steering.

By now he was in a state of profound shock; his knees were beginning to sag but he continued to make his way to the bridge. The captain was in danger, perhaps already dead. If that was true, it was Goggins' duty to take command of the ship, and some way, somehow, no matter what his own condition, to fight her and save her.

But when he reached the bridge, he found to his vast relief that the captain was as yet unharmed.

Captain Robinson looked with horror upon his old friend. "Go into the conning tower, Bill, and lie down," he said. Turning to Hawkins, whose battle duty was to act as talker on one of the J.V. phones, all of which were now out of commission, the captain said, "Go and look after him, Hawkins, till we can get a doctor there."

A moment later a messenger was sent to fetch Dr. Wildebush.

By the time Dr. Wildebush reached the conning lower, Hawkins had already managed to get the commander to lie down and had rigged two lines from the overhead which he'd attached to Goggins' hands. These lines served to hold his seared arms aloft and prevent them from touching his body.

It was only now, relieved for a moment from his driving sense of duty, that Commander Goggins became fully aware of the torment of his own body.

Dr. Wildebush administered morphine, but the pain was still so unbearable that Commander Goggins asked for more.

The doctor looked sorrowfully at his shipmate of whose agony he was so acutely aware. "I'm afraid to, Bill," he said. "Any more might pass you out. We may have to abandon ship. If you were unconscious, you wouldn't have any chance at all."

Back in the wardroom where Commander Goggins had been injured, Lt. Blessman still remained. There was not a scratch on him. He was dead. He'd been killed instantly by the blast.

In Mr. Smellow's room where doors and bulkheads had been blown away, he heard a seaman say, "Will you release me, sir?" He saw that the man had been pinned against the bulkhead by a pile of debris. Mr. Smellow pulled a door off him and the man, in an acute state of shock, walked away without saying a word.

The sickbay, just under the wardroom, was now non-existent. Its deck, which covered one of the 50,000-gallon oil tanks, had been partially blown away. Burning clothing and debris were falling into the oil tank unimpeded. Also, in this section steam was shrieking out of a broken line, scalding everyone who came near it. At first, Mr. Camp set his men to trying to eliminate this steam leak. But well before the job could be completed, he saw that the steam was tending to smother out some of the fires. He called his men off the job and let the steam have its way.

Up forward a strange and powerful and almost mystic phenomenon had come into being. What the men there were seeing, and yet felt they could not be seeing, was that fire wouldn't burn Bull Aschenbrenner and that tons of mangled metal could not shut off his way. Wherever the fire raged hottest, there was this now demoniac shipfitter who had suddenly, in the ship's dark hour, become a person of unlimited power. He fought fire with extinguishers until they were empty and then began clubbing the fires with mattresses or blankets or whatever lay at hand. Nobody knew how the Bull managed to move about at such incredible speed in the dark, smoke-filled compartments, where decks were waist-deep in rising oil and water, and where the broken, twisted overhead thrust down through the dark like bladed stalactites in an inky cave. At one moment the spreading flames would illuminate him on one side of a debris-built impasse beating out a fire. The next resurgence of the flames a few seconds later would show his broad, sweating back on the other side of the impasse wedging mattresses into a broken bulkhead. Wherever he worked men formed around him to help with the job, to be caught up in the vast currents of certainty and indomitability that emanated from this wild, unstoppable and unbeatable little giant.

4

By the time Van Bergen left the bridge, smoke was pouring out of the hollow tripod legs like chimneys, all, that is, except the one leading up from Central Station which was, strangely, smokeless. And since the first thing to do in a fire is to cut out any air that might be reaching it, a signalman wrapped these openings tightly with canvas. This Van Bergen noted as he started below.

The first man he met was a ship's cook called Pop. Pop looked fine except that he appeared to have a cocoanut on his right breast under his shirt where he'd been hit by a flying powder tank. He was not in pain but worried. Van Bergen touched this spot and it was soft. Thinking it must be air lodged there through ruptured ribs and lungs, he took Pop to the exec's cabin and made him lie down. Van Bergen then headed down toward what was known as "wardroom country."

Here everything was a burning shamble and hidden in smoke and fire and hissing steam from broken steam lines. It was almost impossible for him to tell where he was because the things he had always used as landmarks—rooms, offices, tables, everything—had been blown away. Drury had taken charge here, so Van Bergen went on below to warrant officers' country on the first platform deck where he found himself knee-deep in oil and water. Here the most disquieting thing that he found was that water and oil were coming into the ship not only from below but from various vents overhead, which could only mean that the *Marblehead*, still running and fighting at high speed, must have some scoop-shaped hole in her bottom that was forcing the water in under high pressure. Yet to slow her would only make her a better target for the still-attacking Japanese.

Lieutenants Pierce and Blasdel were in charge of the party struggling here against fire and flood and were doing the best that could be done under the circumstances. Van Bergen, whose aim was to locate the most serious damage and then to concentrate on that, started aft.

The fires and smoke and twisted steel in wardroom country made it impossible to go aft through the ship. He started up and over.

Once outside he could see how acute was the ship's list to starboard, and how badly she was down by the head. Already at the bow her normal waterline had dropped fifteen feet below the surface. Everywhere her decks were covered with oil, and men were running from sand lockers with buckets of sand to throw on deck so that traffic could move over them.

As he reached the after con, the auxiliary control station, which was the executive officer's battle station, he thought, because of Commander Goggins' condition, that it must certainly have been blown away. But when he got there, he found to his surprise that the station was undamaged. A fire controlman told Van Bergen that Commander Goggins had been injured in the wardroom at the same time Lt. Blessman was killed.

Van Bergen, who until now had not known that his friend was dead, was deeply shocked. "Christ!" he thought. "There's one less good man to bear a hand in this awful mess." But at the same time, he knew he dared not let the seaman see how he felt.

"I had expected to see your station shot up," Van Bergen said.

"We ain't had any trouble at all," the fire controlman said. Then, pointing aft, he said, "But wait till you see what's happened to the fantail."

A few steps carried Van Bergen to a point where he could see the fantail. The deck was gone. In its place there was only a gaping hole and curls of twisted steel. The guns were crazily awry. Billows of smoke and tongues of flame were roaring skyward. It would have been bad enough had such damage occurred anywhere on the ship. But Van Bergen would rather have had her bow blown off completely than have this injury to her stern from which both power and steering emanated. When he thought of what must have happened to her steering gear, he was sick inside and started running. Overhead the air battle was still going on. But that was Captain Robinson's fight. Van Bergen's battle was, along with Drury, to save the ship, now that Commander Goggins was out of action.

Some minutes earlier, when the stern had been hit, the explosion had occurred in the hand steering room, below the C.P.O. quarters and only a few feet away from the after-twin barbette. Paul Martinek was the turret captain and the petty officer in charge. But inasmuch as the sides of the circular barbette, which composed the turret's handling room, were made of armor and heavier metal than the surrounding decks and bulkheads, the force of the explosion had spent itself by dishing out the sides and blowing away these thinner obstacles to the full expansion of its gases. Immediately Martinek had turned the sprinklers on his ready powder and got his men and himself out of the turret.

The barbette ran perpendicularly through the chiefs' quarters. Several chiefs and a number of ammunition passers who had been working here when the bomb burst below them were now either dead or wandering about blinded, their skin dropping off, and vomiting in violent nausea. One of the people working here had been Fook Liang, the sullen mess attendant. He was one of the less seriously burned, and he began at once evacuating the wounded, dragging or leading them out of this burning area to the torpedo workshop. Here Dr. Ryan and Connie Brandt, the dentist, Ace Evans, Starling Harold, and other of the hospital corpsmen were injecting morphine, cutting away still smoldering clothing, and smearing charred bodies with tannic acid and whatever grease was available which would serve in some measure to shut out the air and seal in remaining body moisture. Up on the forward gun deck men were laid out in rows, and gunners, having no tannic acid and not daring to wait for medical supplies, were simply cutting away men's clothing and smearing on gun grease or Diesel oil with paint brushes.

But back in the chiefs' quarters, from which Fook Liang had dragged the wounded, a huge fire was now raging. In racks and on mess tables in the C.P.O. quarters there were eighteen cans of ready powder for use in the 6-inch guns. It had been put there so that the after twin could open fire quickly without having to wait until the magazines should be fully manned and the ammunition train started. The destructive power in this concentration of explosives was more than sufficient to blow the entire stern off the ship. It lay pinned down by a mass of hot steel debris amid a dozen burning mattresses.

Now Paul Martinek remembered that powder. It was up to him as the senior man present and in action in that part of the ship to do something about it. He had two choices. He could run to the forward end of the ship, so as not to be killed when the stern blew off, and hope to be picked out of the sea by another ship. With an incalculably greater risk to himself he could go down into the fire and try, by some means, to prevent the explosion which could very logically occur at any second now.

He started below. Seaman Second Class Claude Becker, who was an extremely powerful man, was right after him. When they had made their way through the burning shambles to the deck that formed the overhead to the magazines, they found that the heavy steel hatch, which by now was almost red-hot, had been sprung. Martinek could not budge it. Becker said, "Let me try it."

He wrapped his hands with rags, took hold of the smoking hatch cover, straightened his back, and started pulling. Martinek watched his face so that, if he tore his own entrails out, he could catch him.

The hatch gave a little. Agony was cutting deep into Becker's face. The rags on his hands were smoking. But the hatch cover continued to move. Finally, it was open a foot and a half. Then with Martinek helping, the hatch was propped open.

Here everything seemed to be a part of the most terrifying nightmare: choking smoke, fire, broken, twisted steel, the horrible odor of burnt flesh. At every step they might fall through a broken deck into a greater fire below. Yet somewhere in this inferno was a great pile of ready powder. Martinek finally discovered the powder and began tugging at the tanks, each about the size of a five-gallon ice cream can. Claude Becker was by his side working with him. Then they were joined by Shipfitter Second Class Link. But the tanks would not budge. They were locked in the massed metal debris.

There was one last desperate, supremely dangerous chance. Martinek took it.

"Open the cans," he said.

A moment later, their arms loaded with the naked cloth powder bags, the men started out through the fire.

When they reached topside, they threw the powder into the sea. They had taken fantastic risks, had the luck to succeed, and must now undertake the same thing over again.

Yet five minutes later all the ready powder from the chiefs' quarters was slowly sinking to the bottom of the Java Sea.

Then Martinek remembered that the magazine crew was trapped beneath the fires. He started below to try to rescue them. When he reached the magazine hatch and opened it, all below was in almost ghostly good order. The magazine looked just as neat and orderly as it might have looked on any peacetime day. The men reported that their powder had been sprinkled and, at Martinek's order, abandoned their stations and sealed it back up.

Overhead Japanese planes were still attacking, And the *Marblehead*, her rudder jammed, unable to maneuver, was still dashing in the same helpless circle, scooping up the sea with her broken bottom. Her forecastle was almost awash. But while the forward repair party, many of them badly wounded men, struggled to quell the fire and flooding forward, others in the stern were struggling desperately to clear the rudder which was jammed full left and which held the *Marblehead* locked inside a tight circle like a frantic squirrel in a revolving cage.

By the time the fantail fire had been brought under some semblance of control, Lt. Frank Blasdel, Machinist's Mate Dale Johnson, Metalsmith Martin Moran and Quartermaster Lester J. Barre were on their way down into the ram room, which was the lowest and aftermost compartment on the ship. In a hurried conference with Mr. Drury they decided the probable cause of the rudder jam was that the valves and pipe leads in the hydraulic rams had been destroyed by the explosion. Oil, introduced under high pressure, drove the huge pistons in each ram, one of which, in turn, pressed back the starboard rudder post arm while the other pulled the port arm forward. The ram pistons and rudder had been in this position when the explosion had locked them there.

Mr. Drury and the others hoped to remedy this situation by "bleeding off" the fluid inside the rams. This, they felt, would allow the rudder to swing back into amidships, or fore-and-aft, position. Once it reached this position, perhaps it could be locked in place and the ship steered to some extent by her engines: turning her by speeding up the propellers on one side while throwing those on the opposite side into reverse.

But it was by no means certain that bleeding the rams would free the rudder. It was extremely possible that the explosion had thrown the foundations of the rams out of alignment, thereby freezing, through a system of transverse stresses, the whole huge mechanism in its present position.

As Frank Blasdel descended the perpendicular ladder into the steering-gear room it was utterly black except for the arcing of broken cables which now and then caused the chlorine gas from broken batteries to flash into momentary lightning. Halfway down, he felt oil and water encompassing his legs and knew that the compartment was flooded shoulder deep. When he was only a step or two from the bottom rung, a body floated up against him. He pushed it away with his left hand, then stepped off the last rung—and there was no deck beneath him.

Clutching madly at the ladder, he managed to grab it. Then he let himself down slowly with his hands until his feet finally met the down-blown deck.

Johnson and Moran followed immediately and, very soon, Chief Electrician's Mate Ritter and Shipfitter Second Class Link.

Hardly had these men started to work when the word was passed that another bombing run on the ship was beginning. At this point Johnson, pushing away the bodies, was about to pull himself beneath the water in order to grapple with and try to remove the forward drain plugs. There was no time to wait, no cover to seek. He knew that if the ship received another hit in any point, she would break in two. She was flooded with hundreds of tons of water forward and aft, while her only buoyancy was amidships. She was much in the position of a piece of kindling that is being broken over a man's knee. And what added enormously to this danger of breaking in two was the fact that so many of the transverse bulkheads and decks, which ordinarily served as cross braces to the general structure, were now blown away. All through this midships section, which was the fulcrum against which terrific pressure was being exerted, men were watching to see when she'd start breaking in two.

In many places, decks had been blown out from under stanchions which, designed to support the overhead, now dangled from the overhead with a "holiday" of space between their lower ends and the decks beneath them. For the moment, watching the holiday between deck and stanchion was the working gauge by which men could tell whether or not she was beginning to break in two. When stanchion end came down to meet deck, her back would be breaking.

Back aft in the horror chamber of the stinking, flooded, flashing ram room, Johnson was facing that Gethsemane which confronts all men who are in profound danger. The job had to be done, but the only way he could control himself was to blur his consciousness of where he was by where he wished he were. He thought of his wife. "Johnny," he told himself, "if you ever want to see her again, you'd better get those drain plugs pulled." So as the bombers closed in, Johnson reached down into the sloshing muck, the topmost foot of which was fuel oil, caught hold of a piece of greasy, submerged steel, and dragged himself down beneath the surface, down to where two of his shipmates were blown up under the machinery, to grapple for the drainage plugs.

5

The improvised sickbay in the torpedo workshop on the main deck was no sickbay at all, but merely a collecting point where wounded men were laid out on such bunks as were available, but principally on the deck, which was heavily coated with fuel oil. "Sickbay" had spread to the adjacent space around the emptied gasoline tanks and aft into the next compartment, which was smoky, dirty, but undamaged. The only light available to the doctors in the otherwise dark compartment was from flashlights. A good many of the pipe-bunks, rectangles of web springs inside frames of one-inch pipe, had been torn from the bulkhead to be used as improvised stretchers by the corpsmen, almost all of whom were performing prodigious amounts of work, with the one rather astonishing exception of Chief Pharmacist's Mate Ace Evans. Once or twice he was noticed almost pointedly avoiding lifting patients that needed to be lifted. What nobody besides himself knew was that his right arm had not only been blown full of small pieces of debris but was also broken. Yet aside from being unable to lift heavy objects, he was working at full capacity, and with an almost magic gruff faculty for making dying men feel that they'd be back on duty in a week and really should be in five days, except that he was allowing two days for goldbricking.

Dr. Ryan was administering morphine to all patients, but focusing additional time and treatment, according to the stern laws of military necessity, to patching up the least seriously wounded first so that they might get back to the guns and pumps and fire hoses. There were no facilities whatever for surgery. Since everything and everybody was covered with filth and oil, he would have infected whatever he touched. There was not enough blood plasma for even one serious case. But though most of the wounded were in great pain, none of them cried out nor complained. Occasionally a man would ask the fellow lying next to him to carry a message to his family in case he didn't make it through. "If you see my wife," one man said, "tell her I love her ... and that I tried."

As the piles of burnt, oil-soaked clothing grew, Fook Liang came back to the sickbay and quietly began hauling them out and throwing them over the side. Oil-covered sailors were constantly, of necessity, running through the sickbay area, and as the oil grew thick on the deck, Fook Liang would attack it with his piles of rags. When there was no fresh water for the patients, he vanished and reappeared with fresh water, but it was hot. Again, he vanished. This time, amazingly enough, he returned with buckets of ice. Again, he went off and returned with a cauldron of hot soup. Nobody knew where he was getting these things. Nobody asked. They just watched in wonderment as the miracles accrued. Between trips he would reattack the hopeless job of clearing the muck out of the sickbay until a passing sailor would bring the news of a new fire that had broken out and he'd be off to help fight it.

Meanwhile Dr. Ryan had broken out a few bottles of the ship's supply of medical whisky. This was administered to all those suffering from shock and frequently eased their condition to a point where they could swallow water. Seeing this, and knowing that all over the ship men who were suffering from wounds and shock were going on with the struggle to save the ship, he went with a corpsman to find these cases and administer whisky where the men were working.

By now, however, those of his patients who had never had a chance began quietly, and wherever it was at all possible, peacefully, to withdraw from the struggle.

Somebody asked a seaman who was running through the sickbay if he had seen the captain and could tell whether or not he had been injured.

"He's up on the bridge givin' 'em hell."

"Well, if Captain Robby's all right," the first man said, "we'll make it."

And a kind of serenity, a hope built in direct contradiction of the facts, a hope based purely on unshakable faith, began to inhabit and permeate the burnt and broken man.

Inside the hollow leg of the foremast where Joe DeLude had become fastened, he had given himself the only wise counsel that could under the circumstances apply. That was: keep calm. Since he couldn't move anyway, he decided to try to think the thing out. Perhaps if he would rest a bit, he might gain strength for one last, demonical, upward lunge that would tear his body through this merciless steel sleeve. On the other hand, there was no way to know whether he dared pause for a second in this struggle. After all, it stood to reason that his battered body must already have begun or would soon begin to swell. There was the further consideration that the ship might be about to drop out of sight in the sea, or that perhaps one spark from some of the fires that were ravaging her might reach the powder which would blow her up.

Well, there was no way to determine these things, but now in his cylindrical dungeon he tried to sense by her roll how much buoyancy she had left. All he could tell from the sensations that came to him of her motions was that they were abnormally slow and lethargic. And by relaxing the muscles in his neck so that his head, the only part of his body that was free to move, could fall to one side or the other, he could determine that the ship had an alarming list to starboard.

Even so, he forced himself to relax his muscles as much as possible, and to breathe slowly and evenly. For several minutes he remained in this state of enforced composure. Some of the ache was going out of his arms and legs. His clothes were completely saturated with sweat. He wondered if that sweat would tend to lubricate the outer surfaces of his clothes or simply tend to make them bind. In any case he not only hoped but was confident that he had lost weight since entering this torture tube.

"Now," he told himself, "if anything does it, easy does. It's the hips that are hung tightest. There must be some way to be small in the hips." He found that it was possible, if not precisely to reduce the overall perimeter of the hips, to reshape them slightly by flexing their muscles. He gave a sharp twist to his pelvis and seemed to reseat his hips in a more complementary location among the bulges inside the mast caused by voice tubes and cables. A bracket, which held these things in place, and which had been digging viciously into his hipbone, now did not press so hard.

Instead of lunging upward in toto, he now tried wriggling one part of his body at a time. He thought that he might be gaining a little. When, after some minutes, his whole body had moved two or three inches, he was able to grasp a higher rung with his hands. Now, still sticking closely to this system of small, ingenious and calculated wriggles, he began to make a slow but reasonably steady progress. And he began to be inhabited by an almost boundless joy. It was as if he had discovered the most priceless secret in the universe. From a practical standpoint, he had. It didn't matter what lay outside that slowly nearing manhole above his head. If he could once more stand free of this steel entombment and look across the ocean at the sun, he could face whatever came afterward.

Five minutes later as he wormed his bruised and battered body out of the manhole that led to the signal bridge, he achieved that wish. Once more he was free and alive. But when he looked about him at the burning, almost sunken *Marblehead*, and the Japanese planes overhead, he wondered if he had much chance of staying that way beyond the next quarter-hour.

Hardly had Joe got his skinned and bleeding body out of the mast when Red Percifield ran up to him and said, "Joe, the midships hit blew up the post office and broke open the safe. I just came from down there. Everything's burning. Your money ... ain't there anymore."

6

The first word that had reached the engine room of the approach of the enemy had been when Machinist's Mate Franklin had yelled down, "Get an arm lock on your steam valves. The Japs are coming!"

Then as the minutes had dragged by while the fighting began topside, there had been nothing to do but wait as men looked about them at the hot pipes crammed with steam which might at any minute be shattered, listen to the roar of burning oil in the fire boxes. Someone asked if it would be necessary to make the hourly report. The reply was that it would not be necessary. Perhaps it would not be necessary to make any more reports at all. This fetched a dry, mirthless laugh.

Then the ship leaped and shook. Everybody knew she was hit. There was no way to know how badly she was hit. Almost every man on the platform started running for the ladder. Surely Lt. Commander Camp would give the order to abandon station. As they reached the ladder, they looked back. There was Mr. Camp, motionless, silent, looking at them. As yet the expression of contempt had not materialized. They knew it would a second later. Nobody said a word. Quietly each man went back to his station.

It had been precisely 10:27 in the morning when the *Marblehead* had been hit. By 10:28 Quartermaster of the Watch Grant wrote in his log: "Heavy list to starboard, eight degrees. Fires forward and aft." By 10:35 word had reached the bridge that the Group Three magazines were flooded. One minute later Grant wrote: "Settling by the head." By 10:44 reports reaching the bridge were more comprehensive. "Damage reported as serious. More settling and listing to starboard, eleven degrees. Still no steering control. Fires below decks." At 10:50, "engineers reported ready to proceed at twenty-five knots. Boilers 7, 8, 9, 10, 11, 12 steaming. Firerooms One and Two secured because of damage."

As early as 10:32 Captain Robinson had sent a message by signal flags to Admiral Doorman on the *De Ruyter* reporting that his ship was damaged. At 10:41 he'd amplified this earlier report by adding that the damage was serious. He had just learned that all the hand steering equipment had been demolished by the direct hit aft. By 10:52 Captain Robinson was attempting to gain some control over his ship by stopping the starboard engines and holding full power on the port propellers to counteract the fact that the rudder was jammed to port. But this accomplished little more than a reduction in speed. The ship was still circling.

And by four minutes after 11 o'clock when Japanese planes were once more sighted on the starboard bow, he ordered all engines full ahead. But for the moment the Japanese aviators had the *Marblehead* precisely where they wanted her: burning and sinking and unable to get away. They would deal with her later. They swarmed down on the *Houston* and released bombs, one of which had the *Houston*'s name written on it. It plunged through her afterdeck and exploded. Forty-five American sailors were dead.

The next attack was centered on the *De Ruyter*, Admiral Doorman's flagship. A stick of four bombs started down toward her, exploded, and hid the *De Ruyter* behind a wall of water. The bombs had straddled her. All four were near misses, so near that most of the *De Ruyter*'s A.A. battery was out of commission. Long since, a message had gone out from the task force reporting that it was being attacked by wave after wave of bombers and requesting that fighter planes be sent at once to the rescue.

There were no fighter planes to send.

Hardly had Electrician's Mate Sevey reported to Walter Jarvis that the I.C. room was gone and had assured him that the escape scuttle was closed and dogged down, than Electrician's Mate Frady rushed up to report that the Central Station was out of commission, gyro wrecked, space flooding, and all light and power out forward.

Jarvis started running forward to try to locate the source of the damage and find out what could be done. He climbed through the wreckage until he came upon Drury and the fire party fighting the fire that was raging in the wrecked wardroom area. As Jarvis stumbled on, a fireman who was tugging on a hose yelled, "Up behind on this God-damned hose." Seeing the hose was tangled in the wreckage, Jarvis stopped to free it and helped drag it forward. Then he was suddenly surprised to learn that he was No. 1 man on the hose. The fire was so hot that nobody could man the nozzle more than a minute or two.

While Jarvis was No. 1 man on the hose, a messenger found him and said, "The captain wants to know the damage to the steering gear."

"Good God," Jarvis said, "is that wrecked too?"

Leaving the hose with the fireman, he went aft as fast as he could. But when he was almost to the stern, he encountered a man who was so badly burned he was blind. He got this man to the sickbay and started back.

After fighting his way past the fire, smoke and wreckage, he had to pause while some other men were bringing a body out. Then he saw it was one of his electrician's mates. He was filled with indescribable horror. It was Tex Owens, one of his very best men.

By the time he was able to get to the space above the steering gear room he found that Frank Blasdel, Dale Johnson, Moran, Ritter and Link were already there, working in oil and water that now reached almost to the overhead, struggling to release the hydraulic pressure on the rams.

Jarvis now started hurrying toward the bridge to report the damage. For the first time he saw that the ship was running in a tight circle and listing badly to starboard, saw smoke pouring from Number 1 hatch and steam spouting from the Number 1 stack. On the bridge he reported, "I.C. room flooded, Central Station demolished, steering motors and controllers blown up, auxiliary steering room completely wrecked, steering spaces flooded, all light and power circuits demolished forward and aft."

The guns were still firing, and empty shell cases were bouncing on deck.

As Jarvis left the bridge and was going aft on topside, the word was passed, "All hands seek cover." He flattened out near Number 1 stack. No sooner had he dropped than he felt something heavy drop on top of him. As he twisted his head to see what it was, a voice said, "That's all right, sir, I'll cover you."

Then once the planes had passed over, the fellow who was covering him got up and hurried away. Jarvis had no idea who it was.

Below decks men were bailing water out of the flooded compartments with buckets, coffee pots, dishpans, anything that would hold water. Chief Bos'n Harvey Andersen was forced, because of his broken foot, to direct this work while sitting on the top deck. "Curly" Annis, a bald-headed young machinist, was on the main deck in water to his knees, with a port open and bailing water through it as fast as he could work. The portable submersible pumps were useless now because there was no electrical circuit to drive them.

After working in the bucket brigade until a seaman came along and offered to relieve him, Jarvis hurried back to the steering engine room. Here men were still fighting the fires and the flooding and were struggling to center the rudder. Electrician's mates were trying to rig makeshift electrical circuits to feed the submersible pumps.

Lt. Commander Drury was here now supervising the damage control work. Jarvis suggested bringing a portable pump from up forward. Mr. Drury agreed, and his manner was so cool and collected that Jarvis, who'd been unable to see how the ship had a chance, was reassured.

He asked for volunteers to go forward with him and get the pump in the forward damage control locker. It was an old-style pump and very heavy. So, Jarvis took eight men and started forward through the hatch that led down to the first platform deck and the pump. As he undogged the scuttle in the hatch he could hear the sound of rushing water. He went through the hatch first and into the utter darkness below.

As he went down the ladder he stepped into water. Turning on his flashlight he could see that it was knee-deep. The men followed and they soon found that the water was pouring in from magazine ventilation ducts and sprung steel doors.

Jarvis ordered some of the men to try to stop the flooding from the vent ducts. Men grabbed the flaps with their hands and held them down until they could be lashed in place with pieces of line, which somewhat restricted the flow. He realized there was no point in trying to move the pump since this area was flooded worse than the stern. He ordered some of the men to set up the pump there and others to try to rig emergency electrical leads to run it.

Jarvis started back aft to report this change of plan to Mr. Drury.

In the flooded ram room, the brutal struggle to free the rudder was still going on. Men nauseated by the stench of burnt flesh and swallowed oil were still dragging themselves beneath the oil in an effort to bleed the rams. The removal of the drain plugs was complicated by many factors. In the first place their location was unfamiliar. Ordinarily it was necessary to remove them only during major overhauls which occurred years apart. But it was necessary for the men to drag themselves beneath the surface even to grope for them. And since the ship was swaying, causing a continual wash of the oil and water in the compartment, and since every piece of machinery was coated in fuel oil, so that a clutching hand was continually slipping off, the mere job of holding oneself beneath the surface was heartbreakingly difficult, to say nothing of the fact that this constant immersion in fuel oil set one's skin, and particularly one's eyes, on fire. Other men rigged two three-ton chain falls on the rudder yoke so that once the rudder was freed, the falls, anchored to the ram beds, could work the rudder into position and hold it there.

The Japanese plane attack had now lasted over two hours. Other bombs, after the *Marblehead* had been hit, had been sent screaming down toward her, but had missed. By now the men in the ram room knew that they'd soon find out whether or not they had any chance at all of freeing the rudder or whether it was permanently frozen, which would mean that, even if the ship could be kept afloat, she could not get away.

As this time of desperate climax had almost been reached, Walter Jarvis had already reported to Mr. Drury and had again started forward. As he passed through the sickbay, Dr. Ryan had stopped him to see if he knew any way of getting water, in reasonable quantities, to this area for the wounded.

It was while he and Dr. Ryan were talking that the rudder was finally freed. The ship rolled from its starboard list to port. As the rudder centered, many wounded men were lying on the deck wrapped in blankets. When the ship rolled, the water that was piled up on the starboard side swept across the ship to port. It swept over the wounded men on deck. Someone yelled, "We're rolling over!"

"I never saw such a sight," Walter Jarvis said later, "as when those men, burned to a crisp, rose to their feet and nearly trampled each other as they tried to reach what they thought would be safety. It was all that Dr. Brandt and I could do to keep them from rushing up to the topside. It was indescribable."

CARRIER USS *FRANKLIN* STEAMS PAST THE *MARBLEHEAD*, IN NEW
YORK HARBOR, C. 28 APRIL 1945.

PART 6

1

AS OF SOMETHING LIKE NOON, several important things had come to pass; among them, that there was no longer so large a ship as a cruiser in fighting trim in the American Asiatic Fleet. The undamaged vessels were a few obsolete, but still fighting, destroyers and some submarines.

It was also slightly after noon on this February 4th when the *Marblehead*'s jammed rudder was worked into an amidships position. A few minutes earlier the Japanese bombers had spent their last bombs and started back to their base for more. All fires on the *Marblehead* were under control. She had no steering control, but her rudder was centered and locked in place. She had twenty-six compartments completely and eight others partially flooded. The water was gaining on her. Yet she was traveling at better than twenty knots. The rest of the cruiser force had gone on ahead, but the *Marblehead* was still screened by two destroyers. Her people could have abandoned her and perhaps speeded to safety on the destroyers. But certain remarks of Commander James Lawrence, U.S.N., on board the *Chesapeake*, June 1st, 1813, were vivid in Captain Robinson's mind, and he was determined to keep up the struggle to save his ship until he floated off her bridge.

His orders from Admiral Doorman were to steam to the westward. In Captain Robinson's judgment, these orders seemed to indicate that, though he had earlier informed Admiral Doorman that his damage was serious, his commander did not completely understand the dire seriousness of the *Marblehead*'s condition. If she continued to proceed to westward, morning would find her somewhere north of the southern barrier of the Java Sea still in easy range of the Japanese bombers. And the oil which was being pumped out of her was leaving a wide and certain track to her.

It was true that the only alternatives to following Admiral Doorman's present plan were extremely dangerous. If Captain Robinson tried to run south and east to Australia, he would have to pass through areas where seas were ordinarily high and where there would be great risk of breaking his ship in two. Too, there were no adequate ports in Australia within radius of his small supply of remaining fuel, nor were there facilities for caring for his wounded or repairing his ship.

The only other choice was to head for Tjilatjap, on the south coast of Java. Here, if he made it, fuel and, it was believed, docking facilities and hospitals would be available. It was impossible to enter Surabaya on the north coast because the *Marblehead* was now drawing more water than the depth of the Surabaya channel. Besides, the Japanese had already demonstrated that this port was not safe from their bombs. However, to reach Tjilatjap, it was necessary to pass through Lombok Strait, between the islands of Lombok and Bali. Currents, equalizing tide conditions between the Java Sea and the Indian Ocean, raced through the reef-strewn Strait at speeds that were, under the circumstances, extremely perilous. It was, perhaps, foolish to think that this rudderless ship, with her bow down so low that the sea was running green through her hawse pipes, could be taken through it at all. But Captain Robinson was in a situation where he was denied the luxury of probabilities. Every chance was a desperate chance. It was a question of making the hard decision as to which was the least impossible. He decided that it was better for him to destroy the ship while attempting a passage through Lombok Strait than to expose her again to the merciless destruction of the Japanese bombers.

Captain Robinson's decision was also predicated upon information received from his department heads. Mr. Camp had reported that he felt the engines would be equal to the task, that there was no immediate shortage of boiler feed water and that there was sufficient fuel, unless further damage should contaminate his present supply. But one of the most influential factors was the doctor's report that unless many more of the wounded were to die, they would have to be hospitalized as soon as possible. This again indicated Tjilatjap. When Mr.

Drury was questioned as to the ship's watertight integrity, he replied that the ship's remaining buoyancy was so slight that he felt it was absolutely imperative to undertake the Strait's passage, if that meant the shortest route to a drydock.

Since the electrical leads to the ship's signal lights had been shot away, Captain Robinson ordered a message sent by semaphore to the nearest destroyer to be relayed to Admiral Doorman on the *De Ruyter*. The message requested orders for the *Marblehead* to undertake the passage through Lombok Strait and to head for Tjilatjap.

Captain Robinson hoped for an immediate answer because he was convinced that it was imperative to arrive at the Strait early enough to make a passage through it by daylight. Not only was the *Marblehead* without steering control, she was also virtually without means of navigation. The gyrocompass had been demolished. The magnetic compasses were behaving in a most eccentric and unreliable way. Navigation would have to be done almost entirely by sight.

And, as the precious minutes of daylight slipped away, Captain Robinson paced the bridge in profound anxiety, waiting for the reply from Admiral Doorman.

As Captain Robinson waited topside with his eyes focused on the destroyer which had relayed his message, watching for some reply from the commander of the task force, Doctors Ryan and Connie Brandt, having given emergency treatment to all their patients, walked out of the sickbay for a cigarette and a breath of air that wasn't rank with the odor of burnt flesh. Both of them were filthy and utterly exhausted. Yet even as they rested a moment and smoked, their whole concern was for their injured shipmates. They talked of those for whom they had hopes and of those for whom no hope could be held.

"I wish we could do something for the Chinese boys," Dr. Ryan said. "The seriously wounded ones don't seem to even want to live. You can tell by the expressions on their faces that they're just waiting to die."

"I know," Connie Brandt said. "It's awful. Even Evans doesn't get to first base with them. It's that hopeless stare that gets me. If they'd just complain or ask for something."

"Most of them seem to feel they're as good as dead already."

Connie stepped on his cigarette. "Say," he said, "I've got an idea. Those boys think more of the officers they look after than anybody else aboard. Why don't we pass the word for each officer, whenever he gets a chance, to come down here for a minute and say something ... I don't know, just something friendly and pleasant to his own boy, show him that he's interested in him? Maybe that would help."

"It's worth trying," Dr. Ryan said as they started back to the sick-bay. "We're certainly getting nowhere with them now."

As the various officers came in, they sometimes had to be warned beforehand to pretend to recognize a Chinese lad whose features had been burned away. But the result was in most cases something less than magical.

However, one thing finally began to react on the Chinese boys. It was the quiet indomitability, the uncrushable peasant stubbornness of spirit of Fook Liang as he worked for and with them. If he said anything designed to encourage these men, it could never be seen in the immobile expression of his face. He just went on working unstoppably, and those who had eyes left to see looked on and told those who had none what he was doing. Unconsciously, determinedly, he was being that most dynamic of morale builders: one who unintentionally inspires by example.

Thirty minutes after Captain Robinson's message had been sent, no reply had yet come from Admiral Doorman. Captain Robinson could not imagine what could be causing this delay. What was wrong aboard the *De Ruyter*? Had his message failed to reach the admiral? Or could it have been garbled in transmission so that it gave a wrong picture of the situation? Or did the admiral have additional information which made the granting of his request inadvisable? In Captain Robinson's mind, his only chance to save the ship and any appreciable number of her people lay in undertaking the passage through Lombok

Strait, but Admiral Doorman might have heard late reports, perhaps of enemy submarines operating in the Strait, or that it had been mined.

Another half hour passed. Still no reply. An hour of priceless daylight had been doubly lost, inasmuch as all that time the *Marblehead* had been steaming straight away from Lombok Strait, miles which would have to be retraced when there was no time to retrace them. Had the admiral been killed in the air attack and was there now some awful confusion aboard his ship?

A third half hour was dragging by, a half hour when each five minutes saved might make the difference between death and life for the ship. Captain Robinson stopped his pacing and said to Navigator Zern, "What can be holding things up, Dick?"

"I don't know, sir."

Then, finally, the destroyer began busily blinking out a message. Admiral Doorman had granted permission for the *Marblehead* to undertake the passage through Lombok Strait, and had assigned two American destroyers to accompany her. They were to screen her from submarines, take her in tow if that became necessary, act as her guides, and, if worst came to worst, pick up her survivors.

At once Captain Robinson ordered port engines full astern, starboard engines full ahead, to set the ship slowly swinging in a huge arc from her westward course to a southeasterly one that would head her toward the mouth of Lombok Strait.

It was late now, very late. It was out of the question to hope to complete the passage by daylight. But the skipper carried her along at the greatest speed her hull would take until the seas began to rise to a height that made her self-destruction certain unless she should be slightly slowed. Reluctantly Captain Robinson ordered her speed reduced, which, in turn, meant that much more darkness while in the treacherous Strait.

2

By the time the *Marblehead* neared the northern entrance of Lombok Strait, sound-powered phones had been strung between the bridge and the engine rooms. These were phones which contained a permanent magnet inside and were electrically activated by the vibrations of a thin diaphragm which was itself activated by the vibrations of the human voice or whatever other sound. Through these phones the officer on the bridge could give steering orders to the engine rooms where, at the moment, Machinist Lon Howard was on duty, supervising the manning of the great brass wheels which sent the turbines from forward to reverse and back again.

Her foredecks were almost awash, which would have made her enormously difficult to steer under any circumstances. Besides, her screws were unfortunately located in extraordinary nearness to her center line, giving them thereby the least possible leverage. Nevertheless, it was felt that her people were gaining practice in steering by engines alone. Now she was yawing only from forty-five to sixty degrees off course.

Then as she was almost inside the mouth of the Strait, a cross current caught her, made her sheer so that a series of waves slammed into her almost broadside, and set her turning. The only recourse open to the people on her bridge was to let her circle completely. To try to back her down was out of the question. The seas would have piled up against and come over her low stern, where all the decking had been blown away, would have flooded her completely and, in all probability, sunk her.

After the circle was complete, Captain Robinson once more headed her into the Strait as the late afternoon began, with the most terrifying sureness, to fade into night.

The two destroyers assigned to her by Admiral Doorman had been stationed on either bow. They were to probe for reefs and send back screened light signals when the *Marblehead* was moving into danger, because her only means of navigation was to follow the fast-dimming shorelines.

Even though the ship was sometimes crosswise in the Strait, the struggle to keep her afloat and a few of her most vital functions in operation never slackened. Men in the bucket brigades worked without pause. Dale Johnson and Martin Moran undertook another huge and seemingly impossible job. Johnson had discovered a steam line forward which, with some repairs, might carry enough steam to drive a pump. He knew, moreover, that there was a huge pump in the engine rooms which was, at the moment, serving no vital purpose. He asked permission from Mr. Camp to undertake the Herculean job of raising this three-and-a-half-ton piece of machinery to the main deck, and to try to move it along the broken, oil-covered passageways to a position up forward where it could effectively work against the flooding.

"If you think you can do it," Mr. Camp said, "fire away."

At once Johnson and Moran began rigging chain falls, lashing them to beams they hoped would hold, and easing pressures and counter pressures against the pump. Slowly the huge pump began to move.

Outside, night had fallen. There were only the stars, the vague, shadowy shorelines outlined on each side, the subdued wink of lights from the destroyers to warn the *Marblehead* when she was careening into danger.

In the pilot house, Van Bergen, who was giving the steering orders to the engine room, had much the feeling of trying to negotiate rapids in a canoe, using a billiard cue for a paddle.

Suddenly something huge and ominously dark loomed up ahead in the Strait. Very soon it was upon them: a blinding, tropical squall that brought all visibility to absolute zero. The *Marblehead* was lost in the rushing currents of Lombok Strait. Except for the totally unreliable compass which now swung crazily beneath the screened light that rimmed its binnacle, there was no earthly way to tell whether the ship was headed for the shore, for the reefs, or whether she would plow into the depth-bomb-laden stern of one of the destroyers.

As the torrents of rain beat down thunderously outside, the silence inside the wheelhouse was acute. The only sound, remote but menacing, which rose above the drumming of the rain was the plangent splosh of the seas rushing through the hawse pipes, high on the point of the bow, that sleeved her anchor chains.

A messenger, who had made his way to the bridge, approached the captain and said, "Dr. Ryan wishes to report, sir, that two more of our men have died."

"Very well," the captain said, and walked to the other side of the bridge and looked out into the encompassing blackness.

For a moment Van Bergen could not help being struck by the eerie orderliness of the pilot house where there were just the three quiet, tense officers and a couple of silent enlisted men, while, below them, hundreds of men were struggling in the muck to keep her from sinking. Though the ship was lost in the squall in the narrow Strait, everything appeared to be perfectly in order in the pilot house except for the quiet and somehow terrifying abnormality that no quartermaster stood at the now useless wheel.

But the central thought in the captain's mind was the fact that the ship's last hope, if this rainstorm continued, would be gone. The long and valiant struggle of all her company would have been in vain. A cruiser, an old one but one that could have lots of fight built back into her, would be lost to the ambushed, retreating American Navy. If she dragged her bottom across a sharp coral reef, she would sink at once. And at this moment, although the men on the *Marblehead*'s bridge had no way of knowing it, a sharp cross current, running in from the right, was taking hold of her stern and beginning, inexorably, to turn her battered stem straight in toward the nearby shore.

Then the squall passed, just as suddenly as it had enveloped them. The light of the stars revealed the vaguely silhouetted shore toward which she was heading. The captain said, "Bring her right to 130°."

Van Bergen in turn called over the phones to the engine room, "Starboard engines, back full; port engines, ahead full."

After she'd begun to swing back on course, Van Bergen, anticipating the extent of the swing to the right to which her momentum would carry her, called over the phones, "All engines ahead standard... We know we're asking a lot. We need a lot. You're doing a great job down there."

"That last yaw was a bad one," the captain said. "Thank God, those destroyers can dodge like rabbits. Try to average 30° further left if you can."

A messenger brought a lookout's report to the bridge. Very quietly he said, "Another black squall ahead, sir."

"Very well," the captain said.

The *Marblehead* was approaching the narrowest part of the Strait. The seas began to grow abruptly higher. Again, they were engulfed by a driving rain. Through the pitch-black darkness, the *Marblehead* plowed on.

After five minutes that seemed interminable to Captain Robinson as he went from window to window peering into the inky darkness, the squall passed.

With great relief Captain Robinson saw that his ship had accomplished the seemingly impossible. In spite of her battered condition, darkness and storms, she had made it through that dangerous Strait. She was now plunging through the heavier swells of the Indian Ocean.

With Lombok Strait safely behind the *Marblehead*, there was still no rest for her weary men. The bailing went on without let-up. Also, by this time the electricians were grappling with a double problem. Until now the men had depended on flashlights and battle lanterns to light their way. But the flashlight batteries were becoming exhausted and what spares there were had been lost below in the flooded storeroom. Some kind of jury-lighting-rig had to be strung. At the same time, the electric motors on the pumps, being old and inadequately water-proofed, were getting water inside them and shorting out, requiring on-the-spot overhauls and time when there was no time, and every pump was needed every second. And by eleven o'clock in the evening, the old damaged electrical cables were beginning to short out and start fires.

The hatches above the fire rooms were under water on the leeward side and were leaking. But since a certain amount of air pressure is maintained in the engine rooms in the interest of fire-box draft, it was not the water that was leaking down but the air that was leaking up.

About one o'clock Walter Jarvis and Carpenter Billman were working below decks up forward, trying to get lights going, and making chalk marks on the bulkhead every ten minutes so that they would have some idea of the rate of flooding. Each time they looked back from their work the chalk mark was gone beneath the water.

Suddenly Billman touched Jarvis on the shoulder and said, "Notice how she rolls."

She was rolling with a terrifying eccentricity. As she started over, she dropped fast, hung for an interminable period, and then, instead of recovering, plowed, bow down, into the sea.

Jarvis looked about him, felt the broken old ship closing in on him, and started running. He didn't stop until he found Van Bergen and yelled, "She's going, Commander! She's on her way down!"

Van Bergen put his hand on Jarvis's shoulder. "You're awfully tired, Jarvis," he said. "You've done a hell of a good job. Now come with me up to the captain's cabin. You must lie down. That's an order."

But as soon as Van Bergen left the captain's cabin, after making Jarvis lie down, Jarvis was on his feet and gone.

Something like an hour later, around two o'clock, Van Bergen went up on the after-machine-gun nest, saw Martinek there and called him to one side. He said, "Martinek, I want to thank you for what you did today. Many men owe their lives to you."

Martinek said later, "He did not say it as a superior officer would to an enlisted man, but as man to man. He said it in such a way that made you feel as though those men might have been his sons or close kin.

"Then he said that since the after-twin mount was out of commission and useless, we would use it to lay the dead in. He asked me to assist in carrying the bodies, to wrap them in clean white canvas and 'with as much dignity as possible to lay each body down and wrap it in an American flag.'"

3

Men inside the ship never knew when dawn came. There was too much work to do, although they were greatly helped by the fact that Johnson and Moran and the dozens who were on the job with them had finally got the big steam pump installed up forward and it was working. But to the men on deck dawn was both relief and menace. At least they wouldn't sink in the night. Yet they were again naked of cover and open to attack by the Japanese planes.

In the sickbay, where doctors and medical corpsmen and Fook Liang had worked all night, a Chinese boy came in. Though badly burned, he'd worked on the bucket brigade throughout the night.

"When is sick call, please?" he asked one of the corpsmen and added, "I don't feel very good."

Jarvis went on deck to ask for work orders from the captain. The captain was standing on the starboard wing of the bridge looking aft. He had not, of course, left his station since the attack started. He was the picture of weary, dogged resolution. Jarvis cleared his throat.

The skipper looked around, smiled, and said, "Good morning, Jarvis. How are you feeling today?" "All right, sir, and you?" "Oh, I'm fine."

"I was wondering, sir, what you'd like the electrical department to do today."

The captain looked over his wrecked ship.

"There's so much to do, Jarvis, I'm sure that anything you can do will be appreciated. ... I suppose the most urgent thing is to try to get some kind of communications to the guns. As it is, we're virtually disarmed. Can the gear be found for such a job?"

"I'd been thinking about that, sir. And since the degaussing cables have been ruptured and are no longer any protection against mines, I thought we might strip wire out of them for phone lines."

"That would be fine. Good luck on the job."

Jarvis saluted and left.

Hing was waiting with a cup of coffee. As the captain took it, he said, "The ship looks bad, doesn't it, Hing?"

"Yes, Captain. I think mebbe so better you get a new one."

Sometime after the captain had finished his coffee and cigarette, a messenger ran to the bridge with the message, just received, that a large flight of Japanese bombers was in the air and headed in his direction.

His heart sank.

"Sound air defense," he said.

At the sound of the bugle blowing out the air defense call, the utterly exhausted men set down their buckets, looked at each other, and started to the remaining magazines to bring up what undamaged ammunition was left. There wasn't much.

The sunken-eyed doctors broke out life jackets and made ready to throw their patients over the side if the ship were hit.

Now the quiet, greasy men were coming out of the magazines clutching long, roped boxes of 3-inch shells. Some had a couple of loose shells in their arms. It would not be necessary to establish ammunition trains. All the usable ammunition on the ship was now in the men's arms.

The ship could not absorb a hit and live. Then let her die fighting. The resolve, from captain to mess attendant, was complete. They had all fought the good fight, fought it unsparingly. Now that there was no longer a chance, they'd stick with the old Ghost and fight her till she sank, until the Indian Ocean closed over her last gun and silenced it.

Chief Shipfitter McCulley, who had several packs of cigarettes, passed them out among his shipmates. If they were going to be smoked, he said, they'd better be smoked fast.

A plane was sighted on the horizon. Fuses were set and shells rammed home in the guns.

On the bridge Sub-lieutenant Luxemburg, the Dutch liaison officer, turned to the captain in utter despair and said, "What are we going to do now?"

Captain Robinson's job was to hold the ship together as a fighting unit until the last.

He smiled and said, "I don't know, Lieutenant. But if I don't know, how in the hell are they going to know?"

Then a strange thing happened. Lt. Commander J. F. Hourihan was bringing his destroyer Paul Jones along some miles astern of the *Marblehead*. She was a four-stacker and, except for being smaller, looked, from a great altitude, very much like the *Marblehead*. And the Japanese, who throughout the attack of the preceding day had not dropped one bomb on the destroyers in their quest for bigger game, now mistook the *Paul Jones* for the *Marblehead* and swarmed above her.

The plane that had been sighted by the *Marblehead* was evidently a reconnaissance plane and its pilot no doubt was a party to this confusion.

Now, as Red Hourihan stood on his bridge and fought his lunging, darting little ship, he gave a radio play-by-play account which came clearly over the *Marblehead*'s T.B.S. system throughout the fury of the attack.

She survived the first run and then the second, while Hourihan kept the wiry little ship doing the dipsy-doodle at thirty-five knots. There were about forty bombers with nothing to do but ride above him and drop their bombs where it would hurt the most, knowing that if they could plant just one, it would be another one of those nice, clean, no-survivor jobs.

At the end of an hour, the Paul Jones was, miraculously, still alive. Finally, over the T.B.S. came the decisive news succinctly worded by the skipper of the Paul Jones:

"Planes gone. Seven runs. No hits. All errors."

During the rest of that day, the *Marblehead*, so far as Japanese planes were concerned, was unmolested.

That afternoon Joe DeLude took the first respite that he had had since the beginning of the attack. Now it had begun to look as if the ship had a chance to make port. For the Service and for his shipmates, Joe hoped she would. For himself, he didn't much care. That money which he'd saved, and which now was gone meant more to Joe than a cushion against the future. It meant a thousand things which he might have enjoyed yet had denied himself: liberties in dozens of ports where he might have gone with the rest of the fellows and whooped it up and had a little fun. Instead of that he'd stayed aboard ship making himself little speeches that weren't particularly convincing, speeches to the effect that when you'd seen one, you'd seen them all—this referring to ports and women and saloons.

Too, there had been his real feeling of responsibility to make some kind of provision for his sister's future. There were such a lot of things a young girl would need that only money could buy: a pretty dress now and then and, well, damn it, a chance in life. The linens which he'd planned to give her, which he'd selected with such care and such a pleasant sense of being a qualified expert in such matters, were now somewhere in the bottom of the ship under water and either burnt so badly or so thoroughly soaked in fuel oil that they'd never be of any use to anybody.

But the linens were, after all, a secondary thing. It was the loss of the money that scooped Joe out, hollow of all hope and desire to go on. It had taken a lot of fortitude and sacrifice to amass that amount of savings from his own small salary, and now it was gone. His body was a mass of pains and bruises, his future empty of a dozen things he'd hoped he might one day do. He was completely miserable and dejected when Red Percifield came across the deck to him and said, "Hello, Joe."

"Hello, Red."

Red stuck something in Joe's pocket.

Joe sat there for a minute looking at the sea flowing past the *Marblehead*'s wrecked hull. Suddenly he gave a start. On his face there came an expression of mingled curiosity, faint hope, and disbelief. He reached in his pocket, pulled out the envelope, and opened it. It was full of money.

A kind of spasm passed over Joe's body. He couldn't believe it. He looked first at the money, then at Red, took the bills out, started to count them, found himself unable to, and looked back at Red.

"Good God ..." Joe said. "God Almighty!"

"Somebody had got to the safe ahead of me," Red said, "and carried the drawers up to the coding room. I found them on a table. And there was your money, safe and sound."

Joe clutched the envelope. "Good God ..." he said again. "Good God Almighty."

Late that night, Chief Shipfitter McCulley stood watching the Bull shoring a bulkhead with heavy timbers. When the job was done, he said, "Listen, Bull, we're in the soup. We need you and if you kill yourself tonight or tomorrow, we'll be in a bad spot. You've been doing four men's work. I'm ordering you to knock off and get some sleep."

The Bull turned around, grinned, and said, "O.K. Why not?"

And with the most lamblike obedience he found a place on deck free of oil, got a lifejacket for a pillow, slept an hour, and went back to work.

At daylight the next morning, February 6th, the *Marblehead*, by now drawing a few feet less water, was met off Tjilatjap by the tugs that would bring her into port, where the *Houston* was already moored. The last the *Houston* had seen of the *Marblehead*, she was burning and sinking. The *Houston*'s men knew what it must have cost in sweat and brains and guts to bring her in. And as the battered old *Marblehead* was towed past her, the *Houston*'s men, who normally would have come to attention and saluted, instead broke into wild cheering.

The response from the *Marblehead*, even though even Captain Robinson waved his cap and whooped as loud as he could, was damp and small, because battle-weary men who've lived so long with death and violence, who've fought hand-to-hand with fire and the sea and won, cannot yell very loud when their throats are closed by the grip of profound emotion and when they are fighting a losing fight against breaking into tears.

4

Since the Japanese were moving, both by sea and land, ever closer, and moving fast, whatever repairs could be made would have to be made quickly unless the ship were to be either bombed to the bottom of the harbor or seized or scuttled in port.

The only drydock in Tjilatjap was a floating one which belonged to a Batavian engineering firm. But it was too short for the *Marblehead*. The drydock was managed by one of the directors of the firm which owned it: a man named Adama Van Scheltema, a resourceful Dutchman who under the circumstances was his own labor boss, engineer, accountant, supply department and whatever. It would be possible, Van Scheltema said, to sink the drydock beneath the *Marblehead*'s bow. Then after slowly pumping out the dry dock's tanks perhaps the *Marblehead*'s stem could be lifted out of the water so that some kind of repairs could be affected. But there was a great probability that the little overloaded drydock might capsize. Such an outcome would certainly result in great loss of life. It was an extremely dangerous undertaking.

Yet not to undertake it was at least as dangerous. The decision, of course, was up to Captain Robinson. Captain Robinson said, "We'll try it." Meanwhile, out on the topside of the ship, the new Executive Officer (Commander Goggins was among the wounded who had been sent ashore) was walking silently, almost blindly around the ship for the third time, speaking to nobody. Now that there was a moment's respite the true desperation of the ship's circumstance had intruded on Van Bergen's consciousness for the first time. In the past there had always been some urgent measure, some vital decision that had to be made at once, to crowd it out. Now he could not help realizing that here they were in the middle of a war with a ship without a rudder. Soon she would be partially lifted out of the water, on a steep slant, and with a constant tendency to relaunch herself stern end to with her stern flooding worse than ever. Worst of all, she was in bombing range of the Japanese, and if they dropped so much as a hand grenade on her while in this precarious drydock, she'd probably capsize and drown all her men.

But there was good iron in Van Bergen. He was the kind of man who could decide that hopelessness was no excuse. Was he not, as a matter of fact, lucky still to be on the job? After all, look at poor Bill Goggins. A lifetime spent for one purpose yet frustrated by disaster and hideous luck the moment the curtain rose on the scene that was to have given real point and fulfilment to his existence.

A quarter-hour later Van Bergen was back at work, smiling, full of beans, encouraging the discouraged, getting the job done.

A big crane had been brought out for lifting off the huge curl of steel that had once been the deck of the fantail. But when the crane arrived, it was learned that the only man who could operate it had left town. The whole mass of decking would have to be cut in pieces small enough for a man to carry. It was disheartening but had to be done.

"Send for the Bull," Mr. Drury said. A few minutes later, here he came, grinning, carrying a 130-pound steel flask of acetylene gas, his helper bringing the tiny torch. He connected the torch, pulled his goggles down over his eyes, and began cutting the deck into small pieces.

Frank Blasdel was over the side in a diver's rig plugging up holes in the bottom of her stern with wooden wedges where rivets had been blown out.

When the *Marblehead* had arrived, she had been met by a Dutch hospital train which had already evacuated the *Houston*'s wounded. One of the first of the *Marblehead*'s forty-five seriously wounded to be taken ashore was Commander Goggins. As the time had drawn near for him to leave his ship, many of his shipmates who had never before felt especially drawn to the commander now realized for the first time how strongly they had depended upon him all these months without ever quite having known it. Since he was an inveterate cigar smoker, some of the enlisted men combed the ship until they were able to get together almost a full box. Another of his hobbies had been tinkering with radios. Dr. Wildebush gave him his expensive Dutch radio.

"Maybe this will help you pass the time, Bill," he said.

A bottle of whisky was also procured and presented to him. Then, as his stretcher neared the gangplank, the enlisted men brought the cigars. He asked them to light one and stick it in his mouth and set the box on his chest. Thus, taking with him every comfort that his friends could provide, he was carried down the gangway.

The next man to go was Dave Hodges from Redlands, California. As his two old friends, Beauford and Ralph Gabriel, said goodbye, they already knew that he would not live to reach the hospital.

When the *Marblehead*'s filthy doctors and corpsmen carried their wounded over the side and delivered them to the immaculate Dutch doctors and nurses, they had a deep sense of fulfilment. Here was everything: medicines, cleanliness, equipment, which they themselves had been unable to give their patients.

As the Dutch doctors and nurses began to reclean and redress the wounds, the *Marblehead*'s medical corps gave data on each case. Then, conscious of their own infectious filth, they stood respectfully aside and at some distance.

After the wounded had been treated and placed aboard the train which would take them to the Dutch army hospital at Djokjakarta, two hundred kilometers away, Captain Robinson left the *Marblehead*, came across the dock and entered the train. To one man after another he said, "We are sorry you won't be with us for a while." With some of the more desperately ill he made little accusatory jokes about goldbricking, since nobody can help a dying man by being morose. In every case, with a dozen different tactful approaches, he conveyed, "You are my comrade and shipmate. I respect and will miss you deeply. Be of good cheer."

Then it was time for the train to leave. Captain Robinson had been in the Navy a long time. He knew how accustomed men become to leaning on "the Old Man." Now these burnt and broken men were being taken away into the interior of a strange endangered tropical country, and the Old Man would not be with them to tell them what to do.

When the train was gone, Captain Robinson and Captain Rooks of the *Houston* sat together for a long while and said nothing—their thoughts with their men who were, through iron necessity, being abandoned in their hour of need.

When the ship had been floated into the drydock, the tedious problem of lifting her bow was begun. Twice as the drydock began to exert lifting pressure on the cruiser, things went wrong, and it had to be reflooded. The third time, with each man on the drydock in imminent danger of death and working very cautiously, the *Marblehead* rose slowly out of the water. The bow came well clear. The stern was still partially afloat. But the keel blocks showed a critical drag sternward, making emphatic the menacing tendency of the ship to relaunch herself.

Nevertheless, for the first time it was possible to learn exactly what had happened on the morning of February 4th.

The damage to the stern was already understood to have been caused by the direct hit of a bomb that had exploded in the hand steering room directly below the chiefs' quarters and which had, among other things, blown an inch-and-a-half-thick armored bulkhead eighteen inches so that it wrecked the electric steering motors on the other side, then bounced back eight inches.

It was further known by now that the midships bomb had first struck the gunnel of a whaleboat which rested high above the deck. This had started the powder train inside the armor-piercing bomb burning and caused the bomb to explode about eight feet higher than it would have if it had fallen a few inches to the left. In that case, it would have exploded inside the 50,000-gallon fuel oil tank, and that would have been the last of the *Marblehead*.

Now as the hull rose out of the water, the bystanders saw a strange sight. The hull had been blown inward over an area twenty-seven feet square. In the center of this huge indentation there was a hole three feet wide and nine feet long which had been blown squarely into the Group 1 magazines, from which belts of fifty-calibre ammunition hung out through the ship's bottom like seaweed. Apparently, a bomb had missed the *Marblehead*'s foredeck, falling about six feet to the left. At the time the ship had been describing tight circles to the left at high speed, so that, as soon as the bomb went into the water, the ship had begun to move over it. The explosion had occurred just as the turn of her hull passed over the bomb. The weight of the sea had remained constant and noncompressible. There had been nothing to give way but the *Marblehead*'s thin hull.

When men were able to enter the Group 1 magazines, each of which housed a different kind of ammunition, they found specimens of each kind blown into all four rooms. Three-inch fixed ammunition (powder and shell in a single unit ready to shoot) were found twisted into the shapes of hairpins and pretzels. Why these magazines did not explode and, at the very least, blow the bow off the ship, no one knew. It is true that a wall of water was blown into the magazines, but there was a fraction of a second before it reached and wet down the ammunition when it could very well have been blown back out. Beyond question, God had been very good to the *Marblehead*.

Admiral Hart arrived by plane from Surabaya while the *Marblehead* was still in drydock. After inspecting the ship thoroughly, Admiral Hart, who always had been and always would be a direct, straightforward man, said what he had to say to the men of the *Marblehead* in less than a dozen words. With the most profound and moving sincerity, he looked at them and said: "I'm proud to be in the same Navy with you."

5

There were no facilities whatever in Tjilatjap to restore the *Marblehead*'s steering. All that could be hoped for was to slam some kind of patch over the hole in her bow and make a getaway before the Japanese came. Japanese reconnaissance planes were overhead every day observing the progress of the work.

Since Van Scheltema had worked the miracle of raising the ship, and since the word Scheltema was uncomfortable on Yankee tongues, the crew called him "Shelter Me," then finally settled on "Jesus" for short.

Jesus had managed to recruit a gang of Javanese workers to help with the cleaning. At the moment, the crew was carrying ammunition out of the forward magazines (which the Javanese refused to enter), so patches could be welded on. The near-miss bomb had shortened their trip. They simply passed it out through the bottom of the ship.

Though the Javanese are small people, these workers were usually quite large by quitting time, since all the discarded, oil-soaked garments they came upon during the day—and the ship was full of such garments—they simply put on. But one of the most astonishing incidents occurred when a Dutch priest came aboard to confess those of the ship's Catholic personnel, since she had no chaplain of her own. The priest, who very much resembled C. Aubrey Smith, did not speak English. But, oddly enough, that seemed to be no obstacle either to the Catholics or to many of the Protestant men. Confession went on for five hours.

During this time other men were out on deck picking through a pile of oil-soaked personal gear, looking, hoping to find undamaged some last link with home. Suddenly Chief Bos'n Andersen yelled, "Red!" Red Percifield looked up. "Here she is, Red, not hurt much either." Percifield went over and looked at the photograph of his sweetheart. The frame was charred, features oil-soaked, and there was a hole through the shoulder, but she was still smiling. "Gee, thanks," was all Percifield could say. He started looking for something to wrap it in. It was the only personal possession he had left.

A less pleasant discovery was made by Electrician's Mate W. A. Patterson, whose watch Tex Owens had been standing at the time of the attack since Patterson was ill. Patterson knew, of course, that his friend was dead. But Patterson's guitar had also been back in the stern of the ship. Now, in Tjilatjap, he found it. All that was left was a piece of the neck sticking out of one of the steering motors.

Most of the Marblehead crew, still working under forced draft despite accruing exhaustion, got an average of about three hours' sleep in twenty-four. But this they got in relative comfort. A Dutch cargo-passenger ship, the Tjetyalingla, was in port. And the captain put his ship at the disposal of these weary, struggling men.

Aboard her there was a chance to get a decent snack. The food situation on the *Marblehead* was still chaotic. All the labels had washed off the cans, and the menu for any meal was more or less unknown until the cans were opened, though it was pretty much of a cinch, and a discouraging one, that a large proportion of them would contain salmon. The *Marblehead*'s supply of dehydrated potatoes had been stored in the after-gear locker, had been flooded, and were now a swollen, and still swelling, overflowing mess.

But there was good food on the Tjetyalingla, and a tired man coming aboard at midnight could, by showing some consideration for the steward's financial welfare, often get a fried chicken and a few tomato sandwiches and a coldly sweating quart bottle of good Dutch beer.

The men could bathe ashore, not in tubs or showers, but by standing on a board and dipping fresh water with a dipper out of square wooden tanks. In the beginning of course the men, unfamiliar with such strange contraptions, tried to climb into these tanks, but were finally convinced by the Dutch that that was the wrong procedure.

One evening during a tropical rainstorm, a number of men on the *Marblehead*, preferring such an al fresco shower to the trough-and-dipper kind, stripped quickly, hurried on deck, and lathered themselves. The rain ceased abruptly, leaving the astonished men covered with soap. After that they stuck to the curious showers ashore.

Yet despite the furious labor that was going on to try to get the ship in some sort of condition to escape the enemy, there were also some fairly delicate matters of personal relations to be dealt with.

When the wounded had been sent off to the hospital, Chang had accompanied Commander Goggins to try to make the trip as comfortable as possible for him. Now on his return he found Wong, Van Bergen's regular boy, in attendance on the new executive officer. Chang said this was wrong, that he was the executive officer's boy and went with the room. Wong said he was Van Bergen's boy and that, though Van Bergen's duties had changed, he was still the same man. Here was a problem in Oriental psychology to which Van Bergen did not know the answer and in which he carefully avoided becoming involved, though anyone would have wanted the incomparable Chang for his boy. The matter was finally settled in caucus somewhere in the bottom of the ship with all the Chinese present. The question was put for general discussion, and after a noisy hearing of all testimony and after very careful consideration, the assembly ruled that Chang went with the room. Wong, to save face, immediately requested duty as a cook in the officers' galley. But, to show there were no hard feelings, he gave Van Bergen a Shanghai dollar as a keepsake and parting gift.

The *Marblehead* remained in Tjilatjap a week.

On the night of February 12th, Captain Robinson wrote, "We are as ready as we can be but that isn't saying much. This place is getting hot."

Water was still pouring into her from imperfect welds made in great haste. But enough pumps were going so that, if she sustained no further damage, had reasonable luck with the weather, did not break in two (which two British officers were willing to bet would happen) and did not get caught by the enemy, she had a chance to make it to the next port. The hole in her bottom was sufficiently closed to keep out the powerful surge of the seas, thereby reducing the chances of a bulkhead giving. A wood and canvas deck had been laid over her fantail. And a large number of bamboo poles had been brought aboard and rigged with lines so that they might serve as life rafts.

Of the events that had occurred when the ship had cleared the dock for the drydock, Chief Bos'n Andersen had written:

"The scene that will, forever, stick in all our memories was the funeral service that was held for the forty-five dead from the *Houston* and the thirteen from our ship in Tjilatjap. It was just before dawn, misty and a bit cool, as is usual in subtropical places. The dead were laid out on the dock in homemade coffins, all of which were flag-covered. Just as light was coming, the Chaplain from the *Houston* started his service; the word was passed, 'All hands bury your dead. Man the starboard rail.' The crew came to the upper deck and took station along the side nearest the dock. It was deathly still, and the Chaplain's quiet voice was heard clearly. About one-third of the way through the ceremony the word was passed throughout the ship, 'Stand by your lines.' The mooring lines were singled up; the Chaplain continued, then from the bridge came the word, Take the tug's lines.' Dawn was breaking and the Chaplain was finishing his service. We heard the command for the firing squad, 'Ready, aim, fire!' The three volleys were fired, word came from the bridge, 'Cast off your lines.' The ship was pulled slowly from the dock as the funeral party carried off our dead on little narrow gauge railroad hand cars..."

As the *Marblehead* slipped out of port, six days later, the crew of a Dutch freighter brought a victrola up to the microphone of her public address system, put on a record, and turned the speaker horn toward the *Marblehead*.

As the Dutch seamen came to attention and saluted the passing cruiser, the record started turning. The music, power fully amplified, went out across the water. It was the Star-Spangled Banner.

The tired men of the *Marblehead*, their skins atingle, their spines stiff and muscles taut, saluted their brothers in arms who, like themselves, were almost without hope but still unbeaten.

Then abruptly this scene changed from one of deep fraternal emotion to one of violent danger. The date was Friday the 13th. Apparently, the *Marblehead*'s luck was gone. The line to the tug suddenly parted and the rudderless *Marblehead* was adrift in the minefield outside Tjilatjap Harbor.

THE WOUNDED FROM THE *MARBLEHEAD* ESCORTED FROM THE SHIP
ONTO A HOSPITAL TRAIN AT TJILATJAP

PART 7

1

WHEN THE TUG'S LINE PARTED in the middle of the minefield, Captain Robinson was aghast, as was the Dutch pilot, who had seen those mines planted and who knew any one of them would blow the ship to Kingdom Come.

"All right now," the captain said, "let's take it easy and try to hold her in the channel with her engines."

The ashen pilot said, "Starboard engines slow astern. Port engines slow ahead."

Meanwhile the tug was frantically making sternway in order to take another line. In his haste, the tug captain brought his boat up against the bow of the helpless cruiser which still had way on. There was a collision. The only forward compartment that was still watertight was torn open.

By this time, it was too late for the tug to take a line and be of any assistance. It was up to captain and pilot to steer her on through with her own engines while the waves washed into this new rupture in her hull.

When she was, at last, safely out of the minefield, Carpenter Billman was put over the side in a bosun's chair to see if anything could be done to cover the hole. But whenever he was lowered near it, the seas beat him against the ship with such violence that, in order to keep him from being killed, and since no repairs could be made anyway, the job was abandoned. And, in company with the American auxiliary ship, Otus, the *Marblehead* set out across the Indian Ocean for Ceylon which lay, by the indirect route to be taken, some four thousand hostile miles away, and with nothing between the *Marblehead* and the Japanese Fleet except the hope of not being caught.

An ingenious device had been rigged which would tell when the ship was beginning to break in two. A long steel rod had been suspended on a hinge from the forward leg of the foremast. A piano wire was then fastened to a bulkhead in the aftermost rod of the midships section and brought forward to the swinging rod and attached, under tension, just below the hinge on the rod. As the ship began to buckle, the tension on the wire would be increased and this long steel indicator would rise, a sight hundreds of men saw with consummate horror in their minds, and prayed God they'd never see in fact.

If the rod moved only slightly back and forth, it would indicate that the weakened hull structure was beginning to "work." This working apart, if slight, could perhaps be lessened by changing the ship's course and reducing her speed. But if the rod should start its upward swing and steadily continue it, that could only mean that the ship was breaking in two, and the order would be given to abandon ship and abandon fast. The men would have a chance to swim over to the accompanying Otus and be picked up.

That was an alternative that gave real comfort to all hands until dawn of the second day at sea when the morning light showed that, with complete silence, the Otus had vanished.

If the merest Japanese destroyer should come up upon the *Marblehead*'s un-maneuverable stern and stay there, it could shoot her to pieces at will and with impunity. But though the enemy was everywhere about, the men on the *Marblehead*, being reduced now to a point where they were almost without protest, simply went about their thousand pressing and taxing duties on the general supposition that the enemy might not catch them, and that if he did, they'd face that problem when it arose.

It was Lt. Commander Drury, with Bull Aschenbrenner serving as his tireless man Friday, who bore the principal responsibility of keeping the ship afloat, though most of the gear originally provided for such a task had been destroyed by explosion. He kept his damage control parties constantly busy taking whatever small means could be taken to make the ship more seaworthy, while Mr. Camp's people worked at extending the emergency lighting and Lt. Tubby Marshall's with communications facilities.

Fresh water lines had to be run to at least a few parts of the ship. Over six hundred men, filthy and busy, cannot be served by a single freshwater spigot in the bottom of the ship. It was a part of the great good fortune of the *Marblehead* that her facilities for the manufacture of fresh water, by evaporating sea water and condensing the saltless vapor, had not been destroyed. Now, as bits of pipe could be retrieved from broken circuits and welded together, sparse fingers of fresh water began to spread through the ship.

In what had once been the wardroom, machinists and electricians were building an ice box out of whatever parts could be found or made. These parts came from the wreckage of the C.P.O. box, the sickbay box, the wardroom box, and the ice cream freezer from the ship's service store. It made the wardroom look like a tenement but before long this Rube Goldberg contraption was actually making ice.

Food still consisted mostly of jumbled, label-less cans and a few potatoes, but a galley had been rigged up that would do to cook in. The officers' galley had been converted into a scullery. There weren't any tables to speak of anymore. Men passed by the steaming pots, had a plateful of food ladled out, and sat down on the deck to eat. Though the food was flat, they ate fast because other men were waiting. There was no longer a third enough mess gear to go around.

Then they went back to work cleaning, clearing wreckage, building, all the while drawing constant and real inspiration from the power and quality of the profanity of Chief Bos'n Andersen, who hobbled about the ship on a crutch like an outraged John Silver, leading the endless attack that strove each day to bring a little more order out of this chaos of crumpled plating, wrecked machinery, and omnipresent black, lubricous fuel oil.

The *Marblehead*, like an animal broken down in conflict, was dragging herself as best she could toward an adequate drydock, the only kind of way station where she could be fully enough remedied to plow on ... where? Home? Almost no one dared think of it. Home lay half around the earth, and there was never any assurance that, by the end of the day, the old ship might not lie, awry and leaning, on the bottom of the Indian Ocean. A mild typhoon, any sort of enemy vessel, could make a drowning man realize what a fool he'd been to have tortured himself with thoughts of home.

But since the mind travels irrepressibly, men found themselves entertaining faint but unkillable hopes of actually, by whatever magic, coaxing the old ship along, of patching, building strength into her, until she might with luck reach home. Of course she had no orders to that effect and might, if she ever reached drydock, be held for extensive repairs, say in Ceylon, Calcutta or Bombay, and be sufficiently patched up to return to the fight, even though one could not look at her and understand how anything short of complete rebuilding would ever make her able to resume her place in the fighting line.

And it was almost with a superstitious feeling of guilt that Chief Bos'n Andersen, for all his driving concentration on the work at hand, could not help thinking of the two fine young boys of his that he had not seen in so long. Even the broad-shouldered Trojan, who was performing miracles in steel by the hour, had been seduced by the thought of how wonderful it would be to get a thirty-day leave and make a bee-line to New Ulm, though his notions of what he'd do when he got there were, at the moment, a sort of wild and happy confusion composed of potato pancakes and fishing poles, of hugging Ma and going hunting with Uncle Joe. It would be the first long leave he'd ever had since he'd been in the Navy.

Down in the steering gear room the heart struggle for the ship's survival was taking place, the struggle to bring the rudder back into active commission before the ship's turbines should, by their excessive use in steering the ship, be destroyed. As Walter Jarvis worked here, he found himself thinking of his wife and the bouncing red-headed twin girls who were now safe in the States and who, but for the grace of God and the stern precautions of Admiral Hart, might still be in Manila where they'd lived until just before the war.

And John Wohlschlaeger, who was in love with a girl he'd never seen, dared think there might be a chance of one day answering the question that had so long tantalized and taunted him: What's she really like? In the flesh? Imagine being there and actually devouring her with your eyes, hearing the sound of her voice, doing lots of things together so that each might see how the other reacted: seeing movies together, maybe taking in a ball game, going dancing. He was violently excited at the thought of taking what had always been a dream into his arms and dancing away with her. At this daring to presume that there might really be some faint chance of his getting home to see her, he was full of a wild desire to go find Joe and ask him all the old questions over again. But Joe was busy, and John was ashamed to ask them for the hundredth time.

On February 20th the Otus again appeared on the horizon and reported by visual signal that, because of the *Marblehead*'s erratic maneuvering, she had lost track of the cruiser in the darkness the first night out of Tjilatjap.

The next day the crew of the *Marblehead* managed to bring their battered vessel into Trincomalee, Ceylon. And there they found that the drydock which they'd been seeking, and so desperately needed, was not to be had. Too, Japanese carriers were reported to be closing in on the place. The *Marblehead*, after forcing her leaking hull almost 4,000 miles with her rudder locked amidships, must, without remedy for her flooding, straggle on and seek another haven.

2

Just before the *Marblehead* left Trincomalee, Walter Jarvis started running to the bridge. For a week he had not gone out of the steering engine room except to relieve himself. He had worked there, eaten there, and slept there, so that when he was needed during the night he could wake up on the job. By now steering motors had been extemporized from parts of other motors that had been wrecked. Pressure lines leading to the rams had been welded together. The rams themselves had been taken apart and washed with fresh water to remove all salt, then baked to remove the last vestige of fuel oil or dampness. As a rust-removing agent, the fluid out of fire extinguishers had, after the gravest deliberation on the part of the captain, been expended in cleaning the rams. This morning, at last, everything had been set to test the steering gear into which so much ingenuity and back-breaking labor had gone. The men were almost afraid to make the test, so much depended on it. But they made it anyway and failed. Despair spread throughout the ship. Then somebody had one last desperate idea for an additional adjustment. The adjustment and a second test had been made, and now Jarvis was reaching the bridge with the news of its outcome.

Captain Robinson turned to the out-of-breath warrant officer and said, "Yes, Jarvis?"

"I'd like to report, sir, that the rudder has just been tested and found ready for limited service."

"Wonderful!" the captain almost shouted. "Convey 'Well done' to all the men who've been working on it." He turned to the officer of the deck. "Call all special sea details. We sail at once."

Half an hour later the *Marblehead*, with all hands now in high spirits, stood out to sea.

What lay before this battered, unescorted ship? Almost all the same old dangers. Yet as long labor-filled day followed day, days of strain resulting from endless work, discomfort and the unceasing pressure of peril, the old cruiser continued to plow her way across the Indian Ocean toward the Royal Dock Yard at Simonstown, South Africa, just at the Cape. Luckily the weather held generally fair, and the fact that the rudder was working again to a limited extent cheered everyone enormously.

By March 13th the *Marblehead* was only some 800 miles out of Durban, South Africa, where she'd been ordered to stop off for fuel. Her 5,000-mile trip from Trincomalee had been largely without incident except for the occasion when, as she entered the Mozambique

Channel, which lies between Southeast Africa and the island of Madagascar, a mast had been sighted on the horizon.

Ordinarily this would not have given Captain Robinson any undue concern, but two days earlier a disturbing message had been received from Admiral Tate, British Commander of the South Atlantic, which applied too nearly for comfort to the situation now facing him.

"Enemy raiders and blockade runners are eluding our patrols. All men of war, including those taking passage, will be held responsible for positively identifying all merchant ships before allowing them to proceed."

Though his guns were still practically useless and they themselves were so little removed from being in a sinking condition, Captain Robinson called for the stranger's identification signal.

Through his binoculars she looked harmless enough, but it was the practice of Q-ships to camouflage their guns as booms and carry torpedoes below the water line. Added to which was the disquieting knowledge that not many days before just such a craft had finished off an Australian cruiser in those same waters.

A second challenge brought no reply from the stranger. Captain Robinson called his crew to General Quarters and, conscious of the damage that might accrue to his ship from the recoil shock, he nevertheless ordered Lt. Marshall, now acting as gunnery officer, to lay a 6-inch shell across the merchantman's bow.

This shot, however, had seemed to be just what was wanted to cause the stranger to run up her identification on the signal yard. She was precisely what she looked, a meek and innocent British merchantman which had, no doubt, for some minutes contained scores of first-class cases of the jitters at the menacing challenge from this unidentified warship.

Then on March 15th, the *Marblehead* steamed into Durban Harbor. The men had been surprised to see the city on the horizon before they saw land. It had reared majestically from the edge of the sea, white buildings shining in the morning sun.

Before the first liberty parties went ashore, some information regarding Durban was posted on the bulletin board:

> The population of Durban is about 275,000, of whom about one-sixth or less are white. The local white population is about 60% of Dutch extraction and 40% English. There is a political faction ashore which takes advantage of improper performances and breaches of discipline on the part of Allied Forces to react against the Allied war effort. The British are particularly anxious that behavior of all liberty parties be of high order.
>
> Not very far north of here is the border to Portuguese Africa. Much information gets to the Axis powers across this border. Do not speak about the action we have been in, damage received or even mention the name of the ship while ashore.
>
> A large percentage of the population is native. It is a criminal offense for a European to have sexual intercourse with any native woman.
>
> South African whisky is double the strength of English whisky and local bootleg liquor is about as near to poison as you can get. Local beer is excellent.
>
> People here seem to collect autographs. The British do not wish you to sign them.
>
> Air Raid Warning: A steady warbling note on the siren. Make the best of your way to the ship immediately upon hearing it.

To the *Marblehead*'s tired men, so long in Oriental tropics, Durban was almost unbelievable: all these white people, and most of them speaking English. While the ship was in port, a British Air Marshal saw Captain Robinson and said, "Your bluejackets are beyond anything, really."

"Something wrong?" the captain asked.

"No," he said, smiling, "but the other day my wife was sitting in her car outside a shop when one of your lads came up, stuck his head inside the car window and said, 'Say, lady, you're beautiful. Will you do me a favor?' She said she'd be glad to if she could. The boy said, 'Just sit there and don't move, willya, lady, while I get my buddy so he can look at you too?'"

"Did your wife mind?" Captain Robinson asked.

"Rather not," the Marshal said. "I haven't been able to hold her down ever since!"

It was also in Durban that the Bull, in all innocence, went back to war. He was in a bar one night and was still thirsty when the place closed. A taxi driver said he knew a place that stayed open all night, and the Bull climbed into the taxi and was taken to a very dark alley. The driver stopped the car, said, "Follow me," and they started up the alley. But they had gone only a few steps when four men closed in behind them. By now the Bull was pretty sure it was a hijacking party. A moment later they drew up with him and demanded his money.

"Sure," the little Bull said, backing toward an alley wall, giving the hijackers a chance to close in. They weren't armed. Why should they be, five against one?

The Bull reached for his wallet with his left hand. His assailants were in close, and he hit the nearest one with his fist and pole-axed him, got another with a sledgehammer blow of his elbow. Now that there were only three, the Jull felt the pressure was off. But he was annoyed that these people should have, in this uncalled-for way, interfered with his evening's recreation. So, he beat the remaining three into a coma, cut off each man's necktie as a souvenir, and went on down the street to try to locate some relief for his now increased thirst.

3

It was on the next leg of their voyage, after the *Marblehead* left Durban on March 17th, that, for the first time since the bombing, the ship's good luck really deserted her.

One evening near midnight, Ski Wardzinski went below to take a regular hourly sounding of the forward holds. There was no reason at all why Ski should have felt any special trepidation about this duty. Someone had done it each hour ever since she had been hit. It was simply a matter of going down into the bottom of the ship and measuring the accumulation of water there. There was also no reason to expect that it was any higher than usual. All pumps were working and, though on the preceding day the sea had been rough, it was tonight reasonably calm. And if there was ever a time when his premonition of death should have been momentarily in abeyance, this was the night.

Another man was with him, but he waited topside while Ski started climbing down the twenty-five feet to the bottom of the forward hold.

Overhead the stars shone brightly as he started down into the blacked-out ship. Once he'd passed below the possible vision of any nearby submarine, he'd turned on his flashlight so that he might see where he was going.

He had neither seen nor felt anything out of the ordinary until he had reached the bottom of the ladder. As he took his first step forward, there was a slightly peculiar feeling in his chest which, with each succeeding breath, began to result in a somewhat pronounced inability to get enough air in his lungs. This might, of course, just be the ordinary stench which had been present here for weeks. It smelled very much like mud flats when the tide had gone out. Every sort of debris had settled into the bilges: boxes of soap powder, lye, rope, fuel oil, food, paint, dozens of other things. The fact that the turbulence of the seas on the preceding day might have churned this rotting mixture to a point where it would exude lethal gases never entered Ski's mind until his respiratory difficulty had not only become acute but had been attended by a strange weakness in his legs.

He was already falling when the realization came upon him that his old enemy had slipped up on him in a form that could not be seen and was clutching him. He knew that at all costs he must scramble his way back to the ladder.

But the same fast-developing weakness that had come into his knees had also permeated his hips and thighs and shoulders. Wild desire and terror could no longer be served by his weakened members, his weakly heaving lungs. He was caught, and he knew he was caught, that he'd never get out alive. He tried to call, but a groan was all that he could tear out of his aching, gas-filled lungs. He lay helpless, face upward in the water of the bilge.

A little over a minute had passed since he'd gone below.

Up at the top of the ladder the man who had been on watch with Ski sat down on an up-ended bucket and wished he had a cigarette. Since he couldn't have one now, he thought of how pleasant it would be when, before long, the watch would change. Then his thoughts ranged on to the next port the ship would touch. He wondered whether he would have as good a time there as he had had in Durban. In his mind he saw in considerable detail the various things and events that he hoped to encounter in Port Elizabeth.

Finally, he yawned and looked at his watch. Ski had been below now for almost five minutes.

"Hey, Ski!" he yelled. "You gonna spend the night down there? Come on. Them other guys ought to be ready to take over by now?"

No answer. All he heard was the echo of his own voice in the big empty compartment.

There was something almost alarming in the ensuing silence.

"Look, Ski, this ain't no time for pranks. Come on up, and let's check out. I'm sleepy." Still no answer. "Ski?"

Complete silence.

Panic seized him. He started running for help.

At 11:25 that night, the Bull had been lying on the deck sleeping soundly with his head two inches lower than his behind which was supported by a kapok life jacket. The life vest was hard and too thick, but it wasn't as hard as the steel deck. And the Bull had long since found that shoulder bones don't dig into the deck so miserably as the points of the pelvis do. Tonight, he slept in a pair of oil-stained, thoroughly grimy, once-white skivvy shorts. He hadn't any skivvy shirts, and it was cold so far below the Equator in March. His chest was covered with a stiff canvas seabag and half of an oil-soaked pea coat which had been, for reasons unknown, ripped in two up the back.

Tonight, he lay sleeping dreamlessly. He was young and his body was ravenous for rest. For days he'd had a debilitating cold, but it had been impossible to keep him in the sickbay. There'd been work to do, work that he knew nobody could do better than he could.

Now he was merely a young, sleeping, powerful but completely drained animal. His right leg with heel drawn up almost to his hip rested against the bulkhead which ran up from the main deck to the weather deck. The light brown, curly hair, which spread over his body like pale tobacco over Kentucky hillocks at sunrise, glistened in copper and golden strands illuminated by the dim red battle lights in the companionway.

At twenty minutes to twelve a seaman walked up beside the Bull, stooped down, took him by the shoulder, feeling the while the incredible handful of muscle stretching from the base of his neck to his shoulder blade, and shook him.

No response.

Then inside himself the Bull began to be conscious of the peculiar, awful necessity to lunge out of a hard, bottomless sleep. General Quarters? Torpedoes? You never knew. Suddenly the force of waking touched a kind of funny-bone in the midst of this desperate sleeping and in a flash the Bull woke up, his back at a forty-five-degree angle to the deck, saying, "What's the dope?"

"Nothing, kid," the seaman said. "It's 2340. Time for you to hit the deck. You got the watch, ain't you?"

The Bull grinned. "Sure," he said, shaking his head in an attempt to wake himself up. "I guess I was sleeping kind of hard. In my sleep it seemed like maybe we were going to General Quarters."

"Well, how about you now? Are you good awake?"

"You called the other guys?"

"Yeah. You with that lousy cold, thought maybe you ought to get the last minute of snoozing."

"Got a smoke? I ain't got nothing but these old greasy drawers... Thanks... Mind sitting a minute? I'm kind of groggy. You sitting there'll help me get waked up."

"Sure, Bull. All I got to do now is wait for eight bells."

The Bull lit the cigarette and took a deep pull. His body was aching all over. The smoke in his lungs was wonderful. He knew the aches would go away. They'd damn well better, because he had no intention of humoring them.

"How's it out tonight?" the Bull asked, still orienting himself but orienting himself fast and gaining a positive grip on wakefulness, despite a nagging weakness in the small of his back and the lower part of his thighs which had been there for days now because of this cold.

"It's swell out, Bull. Stars are bright as I don't know what. And that breeze is nice and cool, just right to keep a man awake. Makes you feel swell. Jesus, ain't we got it easy now once we got this thing where she'll halfway float, and right here on the coast of Africa? Anything starts any rough stuff with us, we ain't in the middle of the Indian Ocean, but right here by this good solid land."

The Bull lay back down on his broad, oil-stained back and stretched his legs straight up in the air.

"Yeah, we really got it soft now," he said. "Kind of rough there for a while. But the way it is now, hitting the beach every day or two, it's pretty cushy if you ask me. Just think, pretty soon we'll be pulling into Port Elizabeth. I got to get me some clothes to wear. Regs or no regs, I'm gonna buy me a Limey uniform if I can't get anything else. Seems like I ain't been clean in months."

"We're really a bunch of tramps all right. Say, Bull, it's a quarter to twelve."

With a nice resilient bounce, the Bull hit the deck feet first.

"Let's go drink a cup of mud," the Bull said, stepping into his shoes. "I don't know what it is, but I ain't got much vinegar tonight. Maybe that mud'll perk me up."

The two men went to the coffee pot, took half-inch-thick, handleless, white cups out of the racks beside it, filled them three-quarters full of coffee, green-black like creosote, poured condensed milk into the cups, then spooned sugar in and went over and sat down on benches on either side of the paintless, scrubbed-board table.

Again, cigarettes were lit. The Bull drew the smoke into his big lungs with eighty-five percent savor, the fifteen percent detraction from a perfect draw resulting from the habit that non-cellophane-wrapped sea-stores cigarettes have of drying out.

His companion looked at his watch.

"What time is it?" the Bull asked.

"Twelve and a half minutes until."

"O.K. I got two and a half minutes more... So, you say it's a swell night?"

"Really swell. The old Ghost is slipping right along just like she had a solid bottom, all pumps working, and, I hope, U. S. bound."

The Bull grinned. Now he was feeling entirely awake, and good.

"You know," he said, "I feel swell. Maybe we haven't got much sense, but we didn't let those dirty bastards get the old Ghost down. We just messed around and monkeyed around and slammed her back together."

His cigarette was getting short now. He looked down at it and thought there might be two more puffs before it would be too short, and he'd have to snuff it out and go on watch.

"I guess we did all right," his friend said. "If we'd stalled around much, she might have gone on down."

"Sure, she would," the Bull said. "We just got in a weaving way. This is a pretty good gang that the old Ghost has got, pretty salty Joes. Strictly China sailors. The Nips got all their licks in and yet this gang turned to and, when the ocean came into her, by God, we threw it right back out... I guess it won't matter much, whatever happens to us after this. I guess this is about the biggest thing a fellow could go through... I never felt any better about anything in my life. They had us stretched across a tub. We really never had no chance at all but by God we made one. And are floating her toward home... So, you say it's a swell night. Thanks, kid, for waking me."

The Bull took the last swallow of inky coffee, mashed out the now quarter inch-long cigarette, climbed over the bench and started out.

The man who had been standing watch with Ski Wardzinski was running across the deck when the Bull got topside.

"What's up?" the Bull asked.

"Ski went below to sound the forward hold. Something's got him. I yelled down but he don't answer." The seaman went on toward the bridge. The Bull started running toward the hatch. Perhaps Ski had only fallen and knocked himself out. But there was always the dread possibility of bilge gas. Something had to be done and done fast. If it were bilge gas and Ski stayed down there long enough, he'd be dead.

When the Bull reached the hatch, he started, without a fraction of a second's hesitation, down the ladder. When his feet were on the deck, his flashlight found Wardzinski. The Bull took two steps toward Ski, then things began happening to him. He felt his eyes setting and something putting his legs out of commission. "Ski," he gasped. The air seemed peculiar and stinking and to do him no good. He seemed to require the most enormous breaths, yet the breaths made things worse instead of better. His head felt as if it were made of brass and somebody were beating it with a hammer. The Bull found, to his surprise, that he was on his knees, then on his hands and knees, catching the edges of bilge frames in his fingers. Now he was simply pawing, blind, insensate, striving, then a quick winding transition, the last phase of the transition between consciousness and oceanic night.

The man who'd been standing watch with Wardzinski next reached the bridge. The officer of the deck, thinking immediately of the possibility of bilge gas, ordered the boatswain's mate to call away the Fire and Rescue Party, which would rush the Rescue Breathing apparatus to the scene of the accident. Messengers were sent to the captain in his emergency cabin, and to Van Bergen, asleep in his cabin below. Half-dressed, Van Bergen started running in the direction of the forward hold.

When he got there some minutes later, neither Wardzinski nor the Bull had come out nor answered when shouted at. The Fire and

Rescue party were in action with Carpenter Billman trying to find a full flask of oxygen among the many that proved to be partially depleted. Realizing this might take some time and knowing that minutes counted, Van Bergen tied a rope around his waist and started below. He reached the bottom of the ladder, holding his breath as he went, and focused his light on the Bull slumped over near Wardzinski. Then Van Bergen's eyes began to set and ceased to see as his legs gave way beneath him.

By now, Billman had located rescue apparatus which, though not in prime shape, would, he felt, enable him to stay below a few minutes at a time—he hoped long enough. By the time he started down, the unconscious Van Bergen was being hauled up by the rope around his waist, and Billman knew that he and the wise and careful use of his equipment were the last hope the Bull and Wardzinski had. He put on his mask and started below.

Once he'd climbed down the ladder, he hastily secured lines around the Bull and Wardzinski and signaled for the men above to pull them out.

When they came up, they were still unconscious, but did have some pulse. They, and Van Bergen, were rushed to the wardroom and laid out on tables as the doctors began working over them, doing everything that their own medical knowledge and ingenuity and the facilities of the ship would permit. There was almost no chance for Wardzinski, because of the length of time he had been below, but they hoped to be able to save Van Bergen and the Bull.

By now the whole ship had heard what had happened and was deeply alarmed.

At one point it was reported that Van Bergen's pulse had stopped altogether. That report was true, but the condition was only temporary. In half an hour or so he came to with a start. Ace Evans was working over him, and Van Bergen tried to climb off the table. Ace held him.

"How are the other men?" Van Bergen asked, struggling.

Ace Evans looked him in the eye and told two lies. "They are fine," he said, "and the captain has ordered you to stay where you are."

The word immediately passed through the ship that Van Bergen was conscious, and everybody was encouraged.

Little groups of men were now standing around outside the wardroom. Fire Controlman Riches was telling about the time in Surabaya when Ski had refused to go to the fortuneteller because he had dreaded having the fortuneteller verify his own conviction that very soon, he would die. "And now poor Ski's in there dying," Riches said, "when that was the one thing that always seemed so terrible to him. He wasn't ever scared of nothing else."

A medical corpsman came out.

Soft voices asked, "What's the dope?"

"It ain't good."

"You mean ... they're gonna conk out?"

"They ought to have done come to by now, if they're coming to."

"Jesus! ... But Mr. Van Bergen made it."

"He wasn't down there so long... Ski's Just laying quiet. Looks like whatever keeps you going when you're unconscious has about been beat out of him. He musta soaked up so much of that gas that it's wilted him down. Looks like it's just a matter of time."

"What about the Bull?"

"It breaks you up to watch the poor old Bull. He ain't conscious and he can't get no air. Looks like his lungs are buggered up some way. He rears clear up on his elbows gasping like if he could get a little higher maybe he could get some air. He's fighting ... hard. But he ain't winning."

Men moved away from the group to walk over and look at the sea. It had never occurred to any of them that anything could stop the Bull, that poison gas, even death, was big enough to encompass him.

"By God, I'm still willing to lay dough he makes it," one man said in response to nothing but his own thoughts. "Why, damn it all, there's a God, ain't there? He ain't gonna go around knocking off guys like the Bull. The Bull's fought his fight. He fought like ten sons of bitches and he won it. This ain't no battle to the Bull. This is just a little half-assed sideshow. He'll make it, I tell you. There's something in that guy that you can't kill..." His voice broke and he walked off by himself. His shoulders were jerking.

They knew now that while the Bull had been putting that ship back together, he'd welded himself into their hearts more deeply than they'd realized.

"Will you ever forget," one seaman said haltingly as they waited outside the wardroom, "when the rest of us punks was having our girls' names tattooed on our chests in Shanghai? Not the Bull. He had his name tattooed on the floozie's leg."

"Jesus," John Wohlschlaeger said, "don't just stand there and yap about the wonderful liberties we had with the Bull."

"Just a few days ago," Red Percifield said, "the Bull and I were sitting on a couple of bitts back aft. He said he wanted to finish his education and try to get somewhere. But most of all he wanted to get a little leave and go see his grandma. He wasn't gonna tell her when he hit the States. But just go a-helling home and bust through the door and say, 'Hello, Ma,' and hug her."

All over the ship, in officers' quarters and enlisted men's spaces, men talked about the monumental animal goodness and vitality and generosity of the Bull. If he had been wounded and if transfusions would have helped, his shipmates would have joyously given a hundred gallons of blood.

Throughout the night the struggle went on. But the Bull had given too freely of himself too long. A little after dawn the last weak beating of his pulse ceased. Then even the doctors and corpsmen who had so long seen it coming looked at each other in bewilderment. What could not be, was.

When the ship touched at Port Elizabeth, South Africa, the flag-draped coffins of the Bull and his friend were brought ashore. A company each of South African soldiers, bluejackets, and Marines from the Royal Navy marched up as a guard of honor. The Bull's and Ski's shipmates came down the gangway and formed on one side of the coffins. Then a slender man with four gold stripes on his blue coat sleeve came out of the captain's cabin and took his place at the head of the

Marblehead's people. The Bull and Ski were carried by their closest friends and placed upon the waiting caissons. The rest of the men from their own division led the guard of honor. The funeral march began.

As the procession marched on, people on the streets stopped and bared their heads. The sunlight was dancing on the streaks of tears on the faces of the ship's men and officers. These coffins contained the *Marblehead*'s own, men who'd shared the same battle experience, the same everything, so cheerfully and for so long. Now as slow, solemn step followed step, all the Bull's and Ski's friends were struggling to shut out pictures of the past that kept coming into their minds: moments of horseplay, of labor, jointly held notions and dreams of finally getting home, but particularly the cold fact that they were with these friends for the last time. But when the cemetery had been reached, the coffins carried those last few steps and placed above the graves, that fact could no longer be hidden from.

The chaplain spoke his few simple words. But little phrases like "our good and faithful, our beloved comrades" made terrible anguish rise up in the men who stood with bared heads looking at the ground.

Then the bugler began the slow, deliberate, eternally uncompromising notes. The coffins began slowly to sink into the earth. Captain Robinson's face was now covered with tears as he saw these good men who had followed him so willingly and trustingly, yet with such dynamic fury when it was needed. Sobbing was now audible among the men. The bugler, it seemed, would never be able to make the last note.

Then, over the coffins, this alien earth closed in.

PART 8

1

FEW ORGANIZATIONS COMPOSED OF hundreds of men falter in
working for their primary purposes when one individual drops out of
the struggle. But a fighting ship is one of the most closely knit and
highly interdependent of organizations. In excess of a man's duty to
perform his designated function, there are overriding obligations. They
are very simple things: to be of good cheer in inverse proportion, and
without limits, to the fortunes of the ship, and to set an example. It is
within these overriding obligations that the quality of greatness and, if
the word may be used in its sacred rather than its prostituted and pro-
fane sense, heroism lies—heroism not as a purposeful display, but a
natural manifestation of simple human goodness, generosity and courage.

It would of course have been extremely difficult, from a standpoint
of simple mechanical efficacy, to find a Shipfitter Second Class to re-
place the Bull. But so far as these overriding spiritual qualifications
were concerned, it would have been, if not impossible, something very
much less than easy to find a man who somehow depended not entirely upon the ship for buoyancy but who himself bestowed it upon
the ship and considered it his deep obligation to maintain it.

Most of the Bull's shipmates were young. They would go on, live
their lives, have their flings, fight their battles, and none of them would
ever think of him except with strong, hot and surging emotion. Yet the
thing which would always cause a little twisting constriction in the
lower parts of their throats would be the memory of his unlimited generosity.

But life and the processes of life had to go on as the ship made one
more lap of her homeward trek. And since the ship was to be deprived

henceforth of the Bull's two powerful arms and never-sagging back, it was well that she was pulling into the Royal Dock Yard at Simonstown where she could at last be made seaworthy. Here there would be facilities for sealing her leaking bottom and temporarily bracing her internal structure so that she might undertake her trip through the South and North Atlantic to an American Navy Yard to be rebuilt to fight World War II.

The *Marblehead* arrived at Simonstown on March 24th, and when she finally was brought into a perfectly adequate drydock, Captain Robinson and all his officers and men breathed their first real sigh of relief, got the first momentary respite in almost two months. Now they could relax the condition of readiness which had been set in Tarakan the morning war began. Ever since that time half of the 3-inch guns and the A.A. control station had been manned constantly. At night or at any time of reduced visibility half of the 6-inch battery and its control station had been manned. A similar condition of readiness had been set up for the watertightness of the ship: hatches, doors, valves, etc.

Each morning an hour before dawn the men were at their battle stations prepared to meet any surprise attack. The monotony of this had been tremendous, but it had paid off on the day the *Marblehead* was bombed. Now that she was in drydock, all this trying routine of condition watches was, at least for the moment, behind her men.

For the benefit of those who were going ashore at Simonstown, the following information was placed on the bulletin board prior to their arrival there:

> *Simonstown is on False Bay, just around the southern tip of Africa and is located on the east side of the promontory of the Cape of Good Hope. Around the Cape is Cape Town, about 20 land miles from Simonstown. Simonstown will probably be a rather small community but it is expected to have the usual facilities for crew's liberty. Cape Town may be reached by suburban trains and possibly buses. This city is believed to be in excess of 300,000 population, of which*

about one-third are white, and will doubtless afford many of the things we have been looking for.

Almost immediately His Worship, the Mayor of Simonstown, called on Captain Robinson, praised him and his crew for the job they had done in bringing so much wrecked steel through 8,000 dangerous sea miles. A day or two later the captain sent for John Bracken and told him to find the mayor's address so that the call could be returned.

"There will be no trouble about that at all, sir," Bracken replied. "His Worship is aboard every day from eight to five manning a blowtorch."

Since it was such a short trip over to Cape Town, the *Marblehead's* people ranged there just as freely as they did in Simonstown and a good many points in between. And all along the line romance began to bloom like bluebonnets along a Texas lane in April. Most of the men had at least one girl, some several. Fifteen or twenty of the crew even got married. One of these, unable to bear an interruption in the honeymoon, overstayed leave two days. When he returned to the ship, he was, as a disciplinary measure, deprived of further liberty while the ship remained in port. So, there he was: just married, about to leave this part of the world perhaps forever, and yet unable even to say goodbye to his bride.

As a matter of fact, many of the bluejackets were pretty bad about their liberty in Simonstown. Finally, the executive officer clamped down. He called the C.P.O.'s together on deck and told them there would have to be a stop to the men's overstaying of leave. Furthermore, he said the men would have to have good reason for an early liberty (leaving the ship ahead of the regular time) and that application would have to be made to him in writing.

The next day a stack of papers was brought in for the exec's signature. Among those handed him was one that read: "Permission for early liberty requested. Reason: Miss Mamie Smith."

Another man requested early liberty "to get there before my bos'n's mate does."

One sailor, who was up before court martial for being absent without leave, introduced as a mitigating circumstance a pleading letter from a young girl who was begging him to come ashore "just once more so that I may know eternal happiness." At the bottom of the letter was the imprint of two rouged lips.

In Simonstown the *Marblehead* men also made the acquaintance of the Royal Navy's mascot, "Nuisance," when he came aboard one day to look them over. Nuisance was a 200-pound Great Dane. While he was on the quarterdeck the officer of the deck told a seaman to get him off the ship, but after an emphatic growl from the dog, no one cared to touch him. When he had satisfied his curiosity, he left the ship without bothering anyone.

The English had given him an able seaman's rating and sworn him into the Royal Navy. It was his habit to get on the train in Simonstown, crowd someone out of a seat, and ride in to the main station in Cape Town. When he left the train, he went to his favorite pub, barked until someone gave him a dish of beer, then wandered on to the next one. After making the rounds, if he wasn't too drunk, he caught the midnight train back to the base. Otherwise he got into an empty car that would be making the morning trip and went to sleep. Once back in Simonstown, he got on the dockyard bus, took a seat up in front, and didn't move until he arrived at the Yard. But perhaps the most endearing and fatherly of all Nuisance's traits was that if he saw a drunk sailor in town after liberty had expired, he would, provided he himself was sober enough to handle problems other than his own, bring the sailor back to the base.

Yet despite the amorous high jinks of the *Marblehead* sailors and this entertainingly bacchanalian routine of Nuisance's, the ship was eventually back in the water, her watertight integrity restored. On April 15th, twenty-three days after arriving in Simonstown, Captain Robinson took his ship to sea, steaming precisely as fast as his fuel supply would allow her to go.

As one lad, already beginning to feel the tingle of excitement of home, though home still lay many thousands of miles away, said: "The old Galloping Ghost has throwed up her tail and's a-heading for the barn."

2

There is a quality about an *Omaha*-class cruiser which gives her many of the exciting attributes of a J-destroyer. She's got lots of go and seems to have a sort of randy ebullience. When she tucks her little stern down into the water and starts digging, at the same time lifting a bow wave that rises up and covers her forefoot, she not only is a thrilling sight, but is also getting somewhere.

At this time, mid-April of 1942, there were formidable German raiders in the South Atlantic. But now the *Marblehead* with her out-of-kilter guns could look first, and if she didn't want to fight, she could run. She had a newly slicked hull, a little dented but pretty watertight. Under most circumstances she'd have the choice of fighting or running. A kind of symphonic ascendancy of men's spirits was coming into being. Already enlisted men were saying that they'd go to sea with Captain Robinson if they had nothing except a rifle to shoot with, but confidence in their hearts.

On April 23rd the *Marblehead* reached Recife, Brazil. An American man-of-war then in port challenged her. When the so-often-reported-sunk *Marblehead* gave her call number, the other ship signaled back, "Are you sure?" and went to General Quarters. They were convinced the *Marblehead* had long since been sunk and refused to be taken in by this enemy ruse. But before they could open fire, Captain Robinson convinced them that this really was the *Marblehead*, so they let her come in without a fight.

The *Marblehead* did not wait to let barnacles grow on her bottom in Recife. All she wanted there was fuel. Two days later, with her bunkers full of oil and some hastily improvised depth charge racks added to her equipment through the foresight of her skipper, she headed out to sea and northward.

Since the submarines were winning the Battle of the Atlantic hands down, there was some comfort in having the jerrybuilt racks, cradling their six-hundred-pound depth charges, aboard, but they were a jury rig at best and no insurance against real trouble. The *Marblehead* had no escort whatever and still no supersonic gear for detecting the approach of underwater craft. On Captain Robinson's chart were hundreds of pins, each pin representing the reported location of a German submarine. There were too many of them about for his peace of mind. But his crew were not overly worried. They had started out on the assumption that Captain Robby would get them through. He had already proved he could, and they'd have fought anybody who said otherwise. The crew of the *Marblehead* was going home and knew it, all the submarines in the German Fleet to the contrary notwithstanding.

That was the feeling at least until, one morning about nine o'clock, the lookouts all began yelling and pointing, and the officer of the deck turned and saw a submarine dead ahead and riding on the surface.

A fast decision had to be made.

The submarine could crash dive before the *Marblehead*'s gun crews could get the range and open fire, and with the *Marblehead* closing the range, the by-then-submerged-submarine should be able to torpedo her handily and with impunity.

"Sound the general alarm. Right full rudder," the officer of the deck said. "All engines ahead full."

He was going to show that submarine the *Marblehead*'s slender little stern and just how fast she could get out of sight.

In fifteen minutes, during each second of which a well-placed torpedo could have overtaken her and blown her stern off, the crisis was past, and, once the horizon was between the *Marblehead* and the submarine, she turned back north and kept on digging toward home.

Now Broadway was shining bright in her people's minds, as were a thousand kitchens and sofas and beds and family galleries, Brady's saloon, just outside the Brooklyn Navy Yard, hundreds of towns and neighborhoods over the face of the United States. Train rides. "Yes, my ship is the *Marblehead*," and the quiet but positive effect on the fellow in the other seat. Hadn't President Roosevelt singled out the *Marblehead* and the now-sunk *Houston* for commendation in one of his fireside talks, said that the kind of fighting spirit shown by these ships was what was going to bring the enemy to their knees?

Solid days of getting somewhere. The old ship you'd stolen from the Java Sea and the Indian Ocean was taking you home. A pile of out-of-date junk that you'd fought on, been through hell on, and was now getting you home as fast as the newest cruiser in the Fleet.

Most days the weather was bright and fine, and a foaming white bow wave rose to a steady height on her slim stem, embossing and refreshing the initials on the plates welded over the hole where her bow had been bashed in by the tug boat as she left Tjilatjap Harbor. This was the one repair job which would not in the long run prove to be temporary. It had been done at Trincomalee, and since it had deeply concerned the ship's watertight integrity, the welder had felt he had a right to take his time and do the best job possible. Very carefully and with consummate artistry, he had welded the plates over the hole, burning the metal rod so that, once molten, it had flowed smoothly, almost seamlessly, between the two squares of steel. Other connoisseurs of such work looking on had said, "Ain't he the nuts though? He handles that torch like I don't know what." Then when he had finished, in compliance with all laws of serious pride-in-artistry, and no doubt in violation of all sorts of naval regulations, the Bull had signed the job by welding on his initials.

At the moment, the bouncing white spray which churned over the *Marblehead*'s forefoot was now encompassing, now revealing the Bull's initials.

There wasn't any post office anymore but Red Percifield, lying on his bunk, wrote a couple more verses about the Galloping Ghost.

Beneath that skin of rusty grey

There beats a fighting heart,

A heart that keeps her driving

Though her guts are blown apart.

We fought one scrap together,

Yes, it was a nasty mess.

Now we're out to find another

And if we do, I guess I wouldn't want a finer friend.

Her humming turbines said, "Going home. Going home." There were, according to wireless reports received aboard, more enemy submarines between Bermuda and New York than in any other part of any sea or ocean.

Captain Robinson thought: "We've had too much luck and need too much more."

The crew might be going to hell on the blast of a spread of torpedoes. In their hearts they were going home. By now the old *Marblehead* was romping on down the stretch.

John Wohlschlaeger was wondering if Joe DeLude's sister were the kind of girl that would want a big church wedding with a lot of fuss, or just Joe and somebody else for a witness in a Justice of the Peace's office. And then what about the honeymoon? It was too bad that there were so many aspects of all this wonderful business that it seemed just as well not to discuss with Joe.

The last day out the executive officer even had the audacity to get gay in the ship's bulletin for all hands:

Memorandum for the Crew:

We expect to arrive off the entrance of New York Harbor some-time Monday morning, May 4, 1942.

The population of greater New York is approximately 7,380,259.

The currency used is dollars and cents, the dollar being equal to a little less than two guilders. There are 100 cents to one dollar.

Some care must be exercised in engaging taxicabs. A meter is placed in each taxi, which registers accurately the amount owed the driver at the end of the trip. The drivers almost invariably speak English.

For the greater part the street cars run underneath the sidewalk. These are known as subways. The fare is 5 cents.

It will be necessary to be tactful in conversation with the natives. The residents of one part of this area, known as Brooklyn, are particularly sensitive in the matter of criticism of their baseball team.

The gendarmerie, or constabulary, consists of about 10,000 big Irishmen, locally referred to as "cops." It is not advisable to call them cops when speaking to them officially. They do not like to argue while on duty.

There is no recent information at hand as to the venereal condition on shore. More data will be available in about two weeks when a study of the restricted list will have been made.

N. B. Van Bergen, Commander,

U. S. Navy, Executive Officer.

Then night fell. That last night at sea. Sleep? On this sweet-running, genuinely trying ship? When Mr. Camp was figuring fuel supply almost to the gallon for the last ounce of speed? He wanted to get home. But there were also a lot of other people he wanted to get home.

The simple fact was that by now, after what had happened, everybody knew each other deeply, had been forged into a highly special thing.

Then dawn, and finally ... land, a vaguely dark shape on the horizon—a symbol for which 600 men, now speeding back to it, had stood almost all alone, and very, very far out in front, and taken it on the chin hard—and managed by what unbelievable miracle, to get back.

Back? When submarines were lighting the Atlantic Coast with burning ships? Yes, back. With that dark fringe on the horizon they could swim the rest of the way.

Millions of people have come into New York Harbor. Kings. Millionaires. Immigrants coming to a strange and baffling land whose secret was supposed to be surcease from hundreds of fears and hungers. But the one most exciting way to come in is the way that the men on the *Marblehead* were coming. They had taken everything the enemy could hand out, and against virtually impossible odds had made it home. As the *Marblehead* stood into the Harbor, there wasn't an un-shined shoe or a non-singing heart. She was bringing home prideful men who knew they'd pulled their weight in the boat.

It was necessary to anchor in Gravesend Bay to discharge the remaining ammunition. The delay was brutal and seemed endless. The men thought, "Why not throw the ammunition in the river and come on in?" Finally, the job was done, the anchor gotten up, and screws once more turning.

Then, miracle of miracles, here was New York all around the ship, Brooklyn on one side, Manhattan on the other. Just below the Navy Yard the tugs came out, but when the heaving lines were thrown aboard the tug off the starboard bow, the deckhand didn't catch it. He couldn't because he had both hands raised and clasped above his head in waving welcome and congratulations.

The ship was brought alongside the dock, lines cast and doubled over the cleats and bollards on the dock.

On the bridge Commander Van Bergen was saying to himself over and over in quiet, thoughtful disbelief: "We made it."

Captain Robinson started down to his cabin.

By now the telephone lines were being rushed aboard.

"Don't say much, sailors," the officers said. "Tell 'em you're safe and give the next man a chance."

One of the phones was within earshot of the captain's cabin. On his desk there lay a letter awaiting his signature. It was a thing that haunted him, something with which he had struggled so long.

Outside a sailor was saying, "Hello, Mom. This is Eddie."

Captain Robinson read:

Dear Mrs. Aschenbrenner:

Early last month it was necessary for me to request the Secretary of the Navy to advise you of the death of your grandson, Clarence Aschenbrenner, who died in line of duty. He was buried with a shipmate in Port Elizabeth, South Africa.

He thought of the old lady out in New Ulm, Minnesota, who had, minute by minute, reared that brimming and warm and yet somehow cyclonic boy—the old lady for whom the telephone would not ring tonight or ever. How empty was this letter of the tenderness, of the healing balm he wanted it to have.

Outside at the phone Eddie was saying, "Gee, Mom, I just said it was me and I'm in the States and O.K. What you crying about?"

Captain Robinson read on:

"We had served together in this ship for many months. I as his captain deeply share your sorrow..."

Now the sailor outside was crying.

Captain Robinson caught his trembling lip in his teeth, "Oh, God!" he said and dropped his head down on his arms.

The *Marblehead* had come home.

THE *MARBLEHEAD* COMES HOME

Made in the USA
Columbia, SC
29 December 2022

5b9ff290-2ed8-4f5a-8f77-1fcb8db859a5R01